Audition Speeches

for Young Actors 16+

Jean Marlow

Routledge • New York

To Bill Germano

'Thank you'

A Theatre Arts Book
Published in the USA and Canada in 2002 by
Routledge
29 West 35th Street
New York, NY 10001
www.routledge-ny.com

Routledge is an imprint of the Taylor and Francis Group

First published in Great Britain in 2002 by
A & C Black Publishers Limited
37 Soho Square, London W1D 3QZ
www.acblack.com

A & C Black uses paper produced with elemental chlorine-free pulp, harvested
from managed sustainable forests.

Typeset in 10 on 12pt Palatino
Printed and bound in Great Britain by Creative Print and
Design (Wales), Ebbw Vale

Cataloging-in-Publication Data is available from the Library of Congress.

ISBN 0-87830-152-6 (pbk)

Jean Marlow

Jean Marlow LGSM, a qualified speech and drama teacher (Guildhall School of Music and Drama), is also an actress and writer with many years' experience in theatre, films and television.

She began her career at the Palace Theatre Watford as a student Assistant Stage Manager, playing small parts. There she played 'Button' in *Housemaster* and went on to work at the Theatre Royal, Northampton, where she was the young schoolgirl 'Julia' in *Daddy Longlegs*. Even after graduating to 'grown-up' roles she went on to work for The Unicorn Children's Theatre at the Arts Theatre, London, playing the Leading Hen – 'Mrs Short-And-Long' – in *A Fox and His Drum*. It was the first time she had had to sing and dance on stage and remembers doing 'a lot of jumping about and squawking'.

In more recent years she played 'Mrs Ebury' in Tom Stoppard's *Dirty Linen* in the West End, and Doll Common in *Playhouse Creatures*. She also played a leading part, 'Mrs Turner', in the award-winning film *The Little Ones*, and 'Mrs Jiniwin' in the Walt Disney series *The Old Curiosity Shop* with Peter Ustinov and Tom Courtenay. She was recently 'Miss Prism' in the Number One tour of *The Importance of Being Earnest*, and 'Winnie Winger' the stunt pilot in an episode of *Jay Jay The Jet Plane*, a new series for childrens' television.

Her other books include: *Audition Speeches for All Ages and Accents, Classical Audition Speeches, Duologues for All Accents and Ages, Audition Speeches for Men/Women* and *Audition Speeches for 6–16 Year Olds*.

She is Co-Director of the Actors' Theatre School, and it is her untiring search for suitable audition speeches for our students of varying ages and nationalities that brought about these books.

Eamonn Jones
Founder Director
The Actors' Theatre School

Contents

Valerie King BA (Hons) Cert Ed, LLAM (Hons), LGSM
Head of Drama, Laine Theatre Arts; Examiner
for the London Academy of Music

Audition Speeches for Men

Audition Speeches for Women

Audition Speeches for Men or Women

Acknowledgements

I would like to say thank you to the actors, directors, playwrights, casting directors, teachers, agents and organisations who have helped me with this book, and especially:

Brian Schwartz and the Offstage Bookshop, Roger Croucher of the American Academy of Dramatic Arts, Betty Lawson, Alan Ayckbourn, Tim Reynolds, Roland Rees, The Royal Academy of Dramatic Art, Gabrielle Dawes, Anji Carroll, Patrick Young, Vicky Ireland, Sylvia Carson, Tona de Brett, Valerie King, actors Pat Kean, Rebecca Callard and Michael Conrad, Julia McDermott, Rona Laurie, Serena Hill, The Royal National Theatre, Ed Berman of Inter-Action, Jacky Matthews, Tom Stoppard, James Hogan of Oberon Books, Amanda Smith, Samuel French Ltd, Kevin Daly, Jacky Leggo, Matt Plant, Mary Holland, Frances Cuka, Carol Schroder, Heather Stoney, Ellen Dryden, Sheila Killeen, Keith Salberg, Margaret Hamilton and the students of the Actors' Theatre School, my Co-director Eamonn Jones, my publishers A & C Black – and not forgetting my editors, Tesni Hollands and Katie Taylor.

Preface

The Frankfurt Book Fair has always intrigued me. It happens once a year and, although my Editor assures me it is not all *that* exciting, it was here that the idea for this new book came about. 'There is a definite need for a book of audition speeches for the 16+ age-group,' they said. 'These younger actors are being left out.' So I began to investigate – and they were right. There are lots of good audition books for older actors and a few for children from eight to 14 – but the group in the middle is being squeezed out. And yet young actors applying for full-time drama school are urged to present audition speeches suitable for their own age and capabilities, and external drama examinations for the London Academy of Music and Dramatic Art (LAMDA) and the Guildhall School of Music and Drama look for the same thing. Most of the extracts in this book are drawn from characters under the age of 20 and some, like 'Frankie' in *Member of the Wedding*, are under 16 but require an actor a couple of years older to perform them.

Looking through casting requirements recently, particularly for younger actors, it's amazing to see how multi-talented you need to be these days. Many performers in Small Scale and Number One touring productions are expected to be able to sing, dance, play an instrument and even have circus skills. The younger members of the cast of The Good Company's *Hard Times* threw themselves into back somersaults, and one of them swung upside down on a trapeze! So I asked actress and choreographer Sylvia Carson, and singing coach Tona de Brett, to talk about developing special skills. Auditioning itself could almost be counted as a 'special skill' and I have also included some excellent advice from casting directors Gabrielle Dawes (Royal National Theatre) and Anji Carroll (television's *London's Burning* and currently *The Wizard of Oz*, Bristol Old Vic Theatre).

All these speeches have been tried and tested by students from the Actors' Theatre School and presented not only in their End of Term shows, but also at outside auditions and LAMDA examinations – so we know they work!

I hope these books will be helpful both to students and to young professional actors alike, and perhaps be a reminder of the many good plays seen in London and the provinces today – and often too briefly on the fringe.

Introduction

'It's different at different times . . . When you're young, you're just a child being clever. Then it changes . . . Then you get older. When other boys get tall and clumsy. And their voices drop two million pegs. We don't do that. We hang on . . . It's like a baby falling down a well. You've got its foot in your hand and you don't let go. So you're not one thing exactly. You're half man, half boy. That's when you find out you can really do it. And it's amazing . . . You come on stage and everything happens the way it's meant to . . . '

Honey in *Cressida* by Nicholas Wright

Many younger actors reading this book will have attended stage school – some from the ages of eight to sixteen – and already worked in theatre, films or television. Others will have done drama at school, maybe for GCSEs or A Levels and taken part in End of Term plays. So they'll understand exactly how 'Honey', a boy actor who had grown up with The King's Men theatre company, feels. Parents and friends praise you; you enjoy performing and you want to carry on. You don't want to 'let go'!

Of course, everyone knows of someone who, like 'Honey', was in the right place at the right time and was handed out all the starring roles. And luck can play a large part in determining your future career.

I'd only just started working and was given a tiny part in an episode of a new television series. During rehearsals I got talking to a young actress, 'Frances', who was playing a leading part and she started to tell me about her 'Lucky Break'. She was on her way to audition for a part in a West End play, when she stopped to help an old lady who had something in her eye. She knew it would make her late for her appointment but she couldn't just leave the poor woman standing there. So she got whatever it was out of her eye and then found her a taxi. When she arrived at the audition she was made to wait, as several other actors had gone in ahead of her. It was so late it was unlikely she would even be seen. But she was finally called and as she walked on stage there, to her amazement, she saw the 'old lady' she had helped sitting in the auditorium. It was Yvonne Arnaud, the famous French actress and star of the production. Frances auditioned and was given the part. After this, of course, she was in great demand not only for theatre work, but also for films and television.

I've thought a lot about her since I was asked to do this book. Would I have got the part if it had been *me* at that particular time? The answer is 'No'. I wasn't ready. Frances was an extremely good actress and well qualified to play the part. She'd studied hard at drama school and had already played smaller parts in good repertory theatres. She'd worked on her voice and – most important of all – she could be heard easily at the back of a large auditorium.

So it's no good just sitting at home day-dreaming. If you are basing your career simply on luck then you're likely to be disappointed. On the other hand, if you work hard, keep your voice in good shape and try to develop as many extra skills as possible, when the opportunity comes along you will be ready to take it. You'll arrive at your audition, walk on stage and 'everything will happen the way it's meant to'.

Why Go To Drama School?

In the early seventeenth century, young boys were kidnapped by unscrupulous managements, put into lodgings and, if no one turned up to claim them, *forced* to work in the theatre. There they were taught to speak lines, exercise their voices and, after each performance, study new scripts overnight ready for the next production. Today you'd have to pay substantial fees to get anything like that amount of experience. And yet a good all-round training is essential if you are to survive for long in an extremely competitive and overcrowded business.

Drama schools in Great Britain tend to be expensive, so it is as well to look carefully through the various prospectuses, not only to see what will be required of you at the audition, but also to make sure you can afford the school of your choice. Not all local councils – or in the case of students overseas, governments – are prepared to assist you these days. However, some schools are now offering degree courses (BA Drama) and most councils are inclined to look more favourably on these. A few universities also offer BA Drama degrees, but these are mainly academic.

In the United States there are very few vocational drama schools like the Royal Academy of Dramatic Art (RADA) or the Guildhall School of Music and Drama in London. Perhaps the equivalent would be the Juilliard School or the American Academy of Dramatic Arts in New York. Most drama courses are affiliated to universities, such as Yale, and are again very expensive. There are no grants available although you may qualify for a student loan. If you decide to go to drama school there are scholarships you can apply for, or you could approach one of the various Foundations for a theatre bursary.

Tim Reynolds, Principal of the Academy Drama School, Whitechapel, has this advice for would-be drama students.

'Why did you buy this book? There may have been lots of reasons. You could be in a class already, or with a private tutor, and be preparing to do an exam such as LAMDA or Guildhall; or you could finally have made your mind up to

5

enter, for better or worse, our acting profession.

If you know that this is what you want more than *anything* else in the world, and that *nothing* in the world can stop you, then you must be prepared to give everything to it – just as the dedicated future sportsperson knows that they have to train continually. If you want to exercise more control over the ball, or if you want to be the best in your swimming team, you have to keep toning up the muscles and preparing yourself to be the best. As a student dancer or singer must practise for hours at a time, so must you. You have chosen the acting profession. The rules are no different.

So how do you use this excellent book of speeches from plays? Well, let's assume that you have an audition coming up. Perhaps for an amateur production, or maybe for drama school. Where do you turn for speeches? If you're auditioning for drama school, you will be expected to learn two at least. Over the years our experience has taught us that most drama schools require one modern and one Shakespeare (or classical), but some will require a "set" speech to be learned as well. Most of us have got a Complete Works about somewhere, and have either seen or read at least a few of Shakespeare's plays. There are some excellent classical speeches in this book, but what about the modern piece? Here you will find an excellent and well-chosen selection to suit any student actor.

Remember that these speeches are only a section of the play. What has your character done or lived through before the speech begins? What will he or she go on to do afterwards? Once you find the speech that you feel is most right for you, you must buy and carefully read a copy of the play, classical or modern. Look very carefully at the requirements for the audition, and make sure you follow them to the letter. When you get there you must listen to the instructions given, and follow them. The most important piece of advice I can give is: know your speeches thoroughly, and above all, *be on time*.

Drama schools are notoriously hard to get into, as the supply greatly exceeds the demand. They are looking for the right people for their course, so you may be talented but not the right kind of student for their style of training. Rejection is part of an actor's life; try not to be crushed by it and just keep going.

Here at the Academy in Whitechapel we run a foundation course called the Medallion Course – a one-year preparation dedicated to getting would-be actors into drama school. Although not a full training in itself, it prepares students thoroughly for training at drama school while teaching the principles of voice, movement, film and TV work, armed and unarmed combat, etc. They have a chance to perform at the end of each term, and prepare, through a series of tests and mock auditions. They also meet graduate students who can tell them more about the drama school of their choice. This may be the way to go for you, but whether it is or not, I wish you every success in your chosen profession.'

The Royal Academy of Dramatic Art (RADA) auditions between 1400 and 1500 students a year for 30 available places. Auditions are held in London and New York. The Principal, Nicholas Barter, looks particularly for commitment and trainability when auditioning younger (eighteen-year-old) students, 'not just those with nice middle-class voices and a few acting medals taken at school'.

Roland Rees has worked extensively throughout the theatre in the UK. He has directed plays for leading repertory theatres, commercial theatre and the Royal National Theatre, and was the founder and Artistic Director of the Foco Novo Theatre Company. He also directed a new play, *Kit's Play*, commissioned from Howard Brenton for the Royal Academy of Dramatic Art.

'At the end of the day, self-confidence and of course talent are irreplaceable. If an actor had something inside which a director clocks, there is an immediate connection. Different directors click with different actors.

Repertory companies used to be the training ground for young actors. They joined a company for a good period of time and immersed themselves in a hierarchy of age and experience. They may have been to drama school but here, within a company of peers of their profession, they learnt at first hand their trade. In this situation an actor's look had to suit many parts.

Now, no such companies exist within the repertory system. A theatre programme runs project by project, the content of which is as much determined by the definitions of grant and sponsorship applications as it is by the artistic drive behind the programme. In this situation an actor's look is chosen for one specific part.

Nick Barter at RADA explained to me that he changed his three-year course so that actors in their final year almost exclusively acted in plays. Two in each term. The period of training was phased out in exchange for the experience of preparing a part. This was directly in response to the loss of the repertory company.

The commerciality of the business has become paramount, even in the parts which receive subsidy and public sponsorship. Theatre itself has become reconstructed in the form of film and TV. Nick Barter finds at RADA that predatory agents are culling his boys and girls onto their books at the start of Year Three. Many get offered film and TV parts. One, this year, made a film in their second year, presently on release. It is hard for Nick Barter to resist these opportunities for his students, but in some cases he justifiably puts his foot down.

So the audition has become more and more to do with casting for one-off events, particularly for those entering the profession. An actor is looked at as a specific for the auditioned part, the director's view of that part and their interior view of the look of the project.

Which brings us back to talent and confidence, because an actor cannot alter these givens. No more is an actor chosen for their 'company' commitment – indeed they may be notoriously difficult – but for their specificity. And only for a brief duration.

Add to the gloss of the audition this – an actor's bankability, which in many cases involves younger and younger actors, soon after they leave drama school. And remember that a so-called "ugly" actor can be bankable.

Going into an audition
Think
I am good, am good, am good.
But don't swamp the director. Be yourself.
Create your own space.
The director is there to "colonise" the meeting.
Leave a memory.'

Roger Croucher, President of the American Academy of Dramatic Arts in New York, has this to say.

'The general admission policy of the American Academy of Dramatic Arts is to admit all artistically and academically qualified individuals who appear to be mature and sufficiently motivated for conservatory training. During the audition/interview, special attention is given to the applicant's emotional connection to the material and his or her ability to listen in the real-world context of the interview, since good listening is fundamental to good acting. Other criteria include sensitivity, a sense of humour, feel for language, vocal quality, vitality, presence, cultural interests and a realistic understanding of self and the challenges involved in pursuing an acting career.

At the Academy, classical audition material is seen as presenting an untrained actor with an exceptional challenge: to speak lines far removed from everyday conversation – but frequently rich with wit, poetic imagery and exalted emotion – with the same quality of honest, personal connection that is desirable when speaking lines from simple, more contemporary material.

Even though untrained actors may not have the vocal development and verbal skills to do full justice to classical material, they can use it effectively in auditions. They should speak the lines clearly and simply, without false emotions or undue emphasis on perfect speech and vowel sounds, while keeping in mind that the character is a human being with something to say and a reason for saying it.'

Developing Extra Skills

Nowadays it's not enough to go to drama school and hope that when you leave there will be a job waiting for you. Try and develop extra skills, both before and after drama school, that will make you more 'castable'.

Agent **Jacky Leggo** says 'it is much easier to find work for young people who can sing'. And a look at recent casting requirements on the Equity Job Information list confirms this. Many drama schools will ask you to prepare a song for your audition, particularly if you are recalled, and most ask for movement and improvisation at the beginning of the session. It's no good standing up and singing 'Three Blind Mice', as one of my students did. Nobody expects you to be an expert singer but they like to think that you've made an effort to present your song properly. And it is well worthwhile taking a few singing lessons.

Tona de Brett, ARCM, has taught voice productions for many years to a wide range of artists, including classical singers, actors and pop/rock singers. She has taken classes in Musical Comedy at the City Lit and in other adult education centres. Her pupils have included Johnny Rotten, Ozzie Osborne, Paul Young, Val Kilmer, Rick Moranis, Jimmy Nail, Courtney Love, John Taylor, Skin, Basia, Martine McCutcheon, Dido and many more. Her book *Discover Your Voice* includes a CD of vocal exercises and is published by Schott & Co.

'Singing has always been an essential part of the actors' stock in trade. From the court jester to the most avant garde musicals – through elegant operettas and bawdy music hall – actors are expected to handle them all. However, it is not enough to be the possessor of a good voice. You must be able to use your voice skilfully and confidently and therefore it is necessary to learn the technique of voice production. You will then be able to sing many roles and to cope with different situations, even singing through coughs and colds. Of course, if you are ill, ideally rest is best; but there are times when "the show must go on".

Keeping fit is vital. Take regular physical exercise, eat sensibly and regularly, don't smoke or indulge in recreational drugs or heavy drinking. Your body is your instrument after all, and the better you treat it the better your voice will be.

Find a teacher whom you like and whose opinion you trust. You will often hear of a good teacher through friends or through a singer you admire. Your teacher will help you with breath control and tone production and will encourage you to discover the amazing resonances that your voice creates in the body. Good singing *feels* wonderful to the performer and the listener alike.

Warm up with a series of vocal exercises before you practise your songs or give a performance. Your teacher should recommend suitable exercises or you can use various recorded exercises. I have a collection of my own that many people use and enjoy.

Care for your voice with respect and affection and it will never let you down.'

Sylvia Carson, actress and choreographer, has worked in theatres in the West End, all over the British Isles and also in Canada, most recently playing 'Muriel Wickstead' in *Habeus Corpus*, 'Lady Caroline' in *A Woman of No Importance* and 'Fairy Godmother' in *Cinderella*. She has choreographed or been Movement Director for many musicals and plays including *Dancing at Lughnasa* and the English premiere of *Bondagers* as well as producing corporate events. She teaches movement and takes choreographic workshops in England, Italy and the USA.

'Some basic movement training has always been included in drama training but sometimes taken under sufferance by the would-be actors as irrelevant. However, today it is essential. Plays frequently include dance as an essential ingredient of the plot – for example, *Dancing at Lughnasa*, *Stepping Out* – or in a climatic moment such as in *Stones In His Pockets*. Without great physical control you could not be cast in a play such as *Up 'N Under* with its fantastic rugby sequence. Pantomimes, children's shows and music hall require an ability to perform simple steps. A short sequence of ballroom dancing occurs in many plays and in period drama, and even if no historic dance as such is included, a knowledge of it is extremely helpful in achieving the correct style and carriage of your body. So, in these days of increased competition for every part, the more ability you can have in the field of dance, the more your employment potential increases.

You need to know your own body too, and know what is the best way to warm it up for the performance ahead. Any training will help, even aerobics or "keep fit" classes should help stamina and movement. However, it is better to learn a basic discipline and, if you took lessons as a child, to build on and consolidate this. Local dance schools frequently have general classes in tap and ballet for older students, and although ballet might sound daunting it is good for control and basic steps. There are evening classes, societies and clubs for just about everything . . . flamenco, jive, folk dancing (a good source of basic steps), Irish, Scottish, historical dance and increasingly various styles of Indian dance. The more you learn the easier it will be to "pick up" and perform sequences in auditions and then, having got the part, in a production!'

The City Literary Institute in London offers classes in a wide range of performance skills, such as mime, improvisation, singing, dancing, playing musical instruments and *sometimes* even juggling, at very reasonable fees. And it is worthwhile finding out if your local council has anything to offer in the way of drama workshops and tuition.

More About Auditioning

Anji Carroll trained as an actress at the Bristol Old Vic School before side-stepping into casting some ten years later. Having served four years' apprenticeship as Casting Assistant to Di Carling, where she worked on projects like *This Life*, Anji decided to become a casting director in her own right. Over the last three years, among other things, Anji has been Casting Director on *The Bill*, a children's series for Granada and two series of *London's Burning*. She is currently delighted to be working on the Theatre Royal Autumn season at the Bristol Old Vic.

'When adults are making the transition from "child actor" to "grown up" there is an all-important question to be asked: "Is this *really* what I want to be doing now I'm an adult?" The grim truth of the matter is that work opportunities are minimal, and even if you've been successful as a child your good fortune may not continue. Unless you are absolutely 100% sure you want to pursue this career – don't!

If you *are* sure, the next question to ask is should you go to drama school? And if so, where? When? You may feel you can make the transition more easily if you do. Others, especially those of you who have attended full-time theatre schools, may benefit from going later, after a few years in the business. Either way, I am a great advocate of drama school training. I went at 18 and had the best three years ever. However, the process of trying to get there can be slow and undoubtedly expensive. If drama school is the way forwards for you my advice is to apply for as many as possible. The courses and the way in which they are run vary tremendously: by visiting half a dozen or more you will have a clearer idea, not only of what's available where, but of which school's training appeals most to you.

Making the transition is not just a matter of years but also of maturity. Auditioners and fellow actors alike will now expect a little extra commitment/dedication. This shouldn't be a horrifying awakening as it only means one fundamental, yet often

13

overlooked, thing – listening. At Bristol it was suggested to us that "acting" is inaccurately named and that it should really be called "reacting" or "interacting". *Always listen*. By listening to thoughts on the project, character, scene/s, the spoken word and so on you will be able to react in an informed way.

If you are expected to learn a speech for an audition, choose something that is near to you in age and experience and be sure you have learnt it word for word. Get to your audition early – especially if you have reading difficulties and there are scenes to look at. If you have been sent a script beforehand read all of it, not just your part. If you are reading a scene, listen and react with the person/s reading alongside you – probably us, the auditioners, who aren't necessarily Oliviers, though we do try! Remember not to hide your face and look up wherever possible. Never be under-prepared. Be confident but not cocky. And remember: *all* auditioners want auditionees to do well. They're on your side. Don't let them or yourself down.

. . . And finally, *don't forget to enjoy!'*

Gabrielle Dawes is Senior Casting Assistant at the Royal National Theatre. After graduating from Warwick University with a degree in Theatre Studies and Dramatic Art, Gabrielle worked as a theatre director before moving into casting four years ago. Previous casting work includes the Royal Shakespeare Company and freelance assisting in film and television.

'You will probably find that each auditioning experience will be different, to a greater or lesser extent, depending on the Director's preferred working practices and the nature of the piece you are auditioning for. You can significantly increase your chances of doing a good audition by being as prepared as possible, and you can do this by acquiring a range of skills, material and information.

Some directors prefer actors to do speeches at auditions, so it is certainly a good idea to have three or four contrasting pieces, classical and modern, in your repertoire. Choose pieces that you feel play to your strengths, giving you the opportunity to show what you can do well.

However, you are just as likely to be asked to read a passage from the play that you are auditioning for. Usually the

Casting Director will send you the script in advance: if not, go out and buy a copy (if it's published) or, as a last resort, ask if you can arrive early to look at the script before going in. In any event, don't go into an audition not having read the whole script at least once. You want the Director to think you're interested and informed, as well as talented, and there are few things more embarrassing and time-wasting than an actor who is obviously unprepared.

Practise your sight-reading skills as well, for those times where the Director asks you to look at a different or additional passage to the one you've prepared. Lots of people find sight-reading quite difficult, so help yourself by picking up any book, opening it at a random page and reading it out aloud without scanning it first. Practise this exercise often, with a different passage each time, and you'll acquire a confidence with sight-reading that could one day make the difference between getting or not getting a job.

And if you are dyslexic, do let the Casting Director know at the point of setting up the audition. They will then be aware that it would help to get the script to you as much in advance of the audition as possible, to give you plenty of time to prepare.

The key thing to remember about auditions is that we want you to get the job! So turn up in good time, knowing all about what you're being sent for, and as prepared as possible in view of the information you or your agent has been given by the Casting Director. Listen to what the Director asks you, and try to relax and enjoy the audition enough to show a glimpse of the real you – the aspects of your talent and personality that makes you irresistible for the job!'

Out On Your Own

Once you've left the safety of stage or drama school and you're 'on your own', the grim prospect of looking for work looms up – as it does for lots of other students leaving schools, colleges and universities. Auditions can be few and far between and you owe it to yourself to make the most of every opportunity. Some people do really well at drama school, are given a leading role in the final showcase and find themselves a good agent before they've even completed their course. Others are not so fortunate. One graduate told me he was given the part of a 60-year-old 'Butler' in his final show, and what was the use of that! The old saying, 'There are no small parts, only small actors' was not much consolation. And agents or casting directors are more likely to take notice of the actor playing a reasonable part in his or her own age group (although it must be said that playing an 'elderly part', if it's done really well, can be both intriguing to the onlooker and satisfying for the actor).

A sub-editor working for a national newspaper said her Editor once told them that often, the most brilliant students at university did very little after they'd left. It was the ones who were aware that they were not as bright or as beautiful as their contemporaries that did the best in the long run. They tried that much harder!

Many young actors today find work in children's or young people's theatre. A friend of mine played 'Edmund' in a tour of *The Lion, the Witch and the Wardrobe* when he first left drama school – and he was 24 at the time! A lot of thought and care goes into these productions and not only can you learn a lot from them, you are also helping to encourage new audiences for the future.

Alan Ayckbourn, Artistic Director of the Stephen Joseph Theatre, Scarborough, and one of our busiest and most popular playwrights and directors, has this to say about the importance of working in children's theatre.

> 'I immensely enjoy writing plays for children, or really what I prefer to call the "family" audience, because it's probably as hard if not harder than writing for adults. You have to be more

16

aware. Children won't lie to you – they judge you immediately. They can get bored very quickly. Adults are polite people normally and if something is a little boring, they'll sit and watch it and think, "Well, it'll get more interesting in a minute." But children just go, "Boring" and turn round and talk to their friends. All the things that matter in any sort of theatre matter twice as much for children. Good story, good dialogue, characters you are interested in. My imagination really catches fire sometimes! To write for such an audience sharpens your playwriting skills no end. It's affected my adult work, I know. In fact, one such play, *Wildest Dreams* – a quite frightening play – is in one sense entirely a children's play. I'd never have written it if I hadn't experienced the thrills and spills of writing for the younger audience.

The shame in this country, of course, is how little importance is attached to children's theatre. It's appallingly underfunded – the companies that do exist providing quality work all year round survive on a shoestring. There are many excellent writers producing scripts for children but there should be many more. But how can there be when they receive precious little monetary reward and hardly any critical acknowledgement?

Young people are the theatregoers of tomorrow, but if they're never given the chance to see exciting, innovative and imaginative theatre in their childhood, how can they develop an interest in watching plays in their adulthood? If we're not careful, they will be lost forever to television, cinema and all those special effects. They will never have experienced the joy of watching something 'handmade' especially for them in one particular place on one particular day. That's what the "liveness: of theatre is about and what we have got to keep alive.'

Vicky Ireland, Artistic Director of the Polka Theatre for Children, has this to say about auditioning and working for children's theatre.

'When we present theatre for young audiences we demand exactly the same production values as for "adult theatre", so we're looking for excellence in all departments. At the same time, ours is a specialised field of work which expects commitment and respect. We are fiercely proud, so don't arrive with a patronising attitude.

One group we frequently need to portray are children and teenagers, so young actors are often cast. You don't have to "act" being a child, just carry the spirit inside you and let it inform your behaviour. Don't worry, we call upon a whole range of actors so there are lots of other characters you can try for.

Most children's theatre is physically demanding so you need to be really fit and have plenty of stamina. And, because children's audiences can behave in unexpected ways, you must have a real sense of humour and be light on your feet in order to adjust. We are also looking for generosity of spirit – you may well have to be with a small group for some time in testing circumstances.

If you get an audition, the following tips might help you.

- If possible, acquire some knowledge of the company's work before the audition.
- If the play is published you should read it, but as most of our work is new writing, you may not get the chance.
- If you don't have an agent, ask as many questions as you need to before the audition. The basics are: details of character, dates, where performing and money.
- Always be sure to note clearly the address of the audition place, the name of who you'll be meeting and a contact phone number.
- Work out carefully how long it will take to get to where you're going, and always arrive in good time. If you are running late, ring to explain. Don't arrive in a sweat; this might be interpreted as being unfit. Take your time, go to the loo, have a drink of water, etc. Then read the piece of script carefully. Better to get your focus than rush in and feel unready.
- If you're not a good sight-reader, say so. Any auditioner will allow for this.
- Be well turned out. Children's theatre is usually physical, so don't wear high-heeled boots or tight jeans, gorgeous as they may be. Better to wear smart, clean clothes you can move in easily.
- Remember bodily hygiene. Use deodorant.
- Don't drink alcohol just before your audition or reek of tobacco smoke. It's a turn-off.
- It is vital to have prepared a speech or speeches. Choose a

good audition piece that suits you and that you feel happy and comfortable with, not a hastily cobbled piece of children's literature. Remember, we are looking for good actors. We don't judge the piece, rather the performer, and we can cope with four-letter words if there are some in the piece you want to do.

- Have a song ready to sing, just in case – with or without accompaniment.
- Being able to play a musical instrument is an asset.
- Be prepared to improvise.
- Be prepared to do and give more than you expect. If you aren't right for what you've gone for, you might be asked to do something unrelated, to do with a part in the future. Just go with it.

Remember: energy, focus, sense of humour and commitment. Play from the heart and good luck.'

Patrick Young, founder of Streets Alive, a theatre company for young homeless people between the ages of 16 and 25:

'Streets Alive exists to give young people a voice to tell stories of their experience. There is a vital need for such expression, and that is what sets Streets Alive apart from other organisations. The purpose of the company is to empower young people (aged 16 to 25 years) who are socially marginalised by their past or present homelessness.

Always at the centre of our work is the voice of the young person; theirs is the most important voice in the company. Together we devise theatre which reflects and expresses their own personal experiences and positively encourages them to move forwards in their lives. *It is never written down – our text is video.*

Because of this our young people are highly motivated and profoundly engaged with the work at the centre of the process. This makes Streets Alive unique, with young people talking to young people about their experience. Through theatre and conversation, through actors and audience, an exciting interaction takes place where the mediation is more or less invisible. The work is very much about discovering the value of experiences in order to make positive choices for the future.

19

Equipping young people with skills to analyse their own work enables them to become more powerful. They feel profoundly valued in this company, where the work is development, and ultimately it's where you place people in the process that gets results. This allows a young person to be creator, writer, performer and musician.

The work of Streets Alive has two main aims. The first is for the young people working at the centre of the company, and can be divided into three key areas: personal, social and professional development. In personal development we see them develop a sense of their own value and as a result their confidence, responsibility and motivation all grow. We also see them developing in their ability to work with other people; the skills of group work, e.g. cooperation and listening, are developed in the course of the work. Finally, they receive training in various areas of the performing arts and then move on to develop these at college or in the workplace.

The second aim is for the audiences that we work with. The work must be interactive, collaborative and eventually shift the way in which audiences see young people at risk. We work in schools, colleges, hostels and with groups of young people in informal settings such as day centres. We take the work to national and international audiences. Last year we took the company – 10 homeless people and 10 professional artists – to Ghana where we devised a performance about life on the streets for young people there. The aim was to tell, as far as possible, the universal story of homelessness. The piece was performed in Ghana and over here.

Young people are educators as well as being educated. Too often this is missing from the equation. If you see yourself as being oppressed and purely as a victim of that oppression, you are robbing yourself of your own power. By working with Streets Alive the young people start to see their power, hear their voices and see their stories as part of a much bigger whole. This in turn enables them to see themselves differently. To find out more about our work, visit our website www.streetsalive.org.uk.'

Advice From The Actors

Pat Keen played the 'Sergeant' in the original production of *The Passing-Out Parade* (*see* page 102) which opened at Greenwich Theatre in September 1979. She has had a long career in theatre, with roles from 'Margaret More' in *A Man For All Seasons* at the Globe Theatre (now called the Gielgud) to the 'Mrs Squeers'/ 'Mrs Crummles' double in the Royal Shakespeare Company's *Nicholas Nickleby* tour, starting at Stratford on Avon and going to the States. Her film roles have included John Schlesinger's *A Kind of Loving*, a Sherlock Holmes spoof *Without A Clue* with Michael Caine, and *Clockwise* with John Cleese. She has also worked with John Cleese in the TV series Fawlty Towers. Her latest work in TV has been the series *Down To Earth* in which she played 'Addy'. Here she emphasises the importance of reading the whole play.

'It was World War Two. I was eight. It was summer and I was sitting on a gate by the road when I heard shouting. Suddenly two girls in ATS uniform riding bikes and pedalling furiously shot down the road screaming with laughter and shouting ribald remarks to each other. The one in front threw all caution to the winds as she steered with one hand and turned back to shout at her friend. This glimpse showed a "devil may care" attitude freed from the restraint of how "nice" girls should behave.

If you choose this extract, it's important to read the whole play because that "devil may care" attitude runs through it. Besides being very amusing it also shows how it affects "Stokes" – what she does and how others treat her.

I thoroughly enjoyed playing the "Sergeant" and when I first joined the cast we were all taken to a place that made uniforms. Anne Valery, the author, had been in the ATS and was insistent that we should have the right material. She crawled over huge bolts 12 feet wide trying to find the exact stuff, rejecting one after another until with a triumphant "This is it!" she recognised a particularly spiky and scratchy khaki wool. Later in the dress rehearsals we had to get used to the weight plus shirt, bloomers, thick stockings, overcoat, gas cape, gas mask and tin helmet and the heavy ATS-issue leather shoes. On the first night I was standing in the wings wearing all this clobber except for the gas cape, mask and helmet waiting for the curtain call. The scene-dock door at the Greenwich Theatre was open and I saw what I thought was a heavy mist coming in from the park. Then I realised that it was coming from me. It was just as Anne had told us happened after route marches: I was steaming like a horse!'

Michael Conrad trained at Rose Bruford College of Speech and Drama, graduating in 1994. His very first job was playing four contrasting parts in *The Queen and I* at the Vaudeville Theatre, London, followed by a national tour. He has since appeared in various roles for both TV and theatre, most notably in the highly acclaimed play *Talking About Men* at the Oval House. On television he has appeared in *The Bill*, *Rumble* and *The Incredible Sock Monster*. He is also appearing in a series of adverts for 'Oasis', the fruit drink.

'I think it is imperative that anyone entering the profession of acting these days should try and acquire a *second* profession. Acting is a fantastic job but there will be periods of unemployment. This can be both frustrating and soul-destroying. Before I became an actor, I trained as a decorator, so when I am not acting I can fall back on my earlier profession. I also think it gives one a certain grounding and stability which is not necessarily found in this precarious business.

Auditions can be quite a daunting and intimidating experience at the beginning. But the more you audition the better you become at them. Once you become comfortable with them they can be enjoyable – even exciting. Always try to find out as much information as possible about your character, the play and the playwright. If you are auditioning for a play, make sure that you read it beforehand. If you can't get hold of a copy, go to the library. You need to be prepared for the audition and this will give you greater understanding and confidence. If there is no copy available, try to get to the appointment at least 30 minutes before the start to familiarise yourself with the script.

Never go to an audition unprepared! It is very unprofessional. A director may also ask you to improvise or read another character – so be ready! It is also a very good idea to have at least three speeches in your repertoire as some auditioners may require you to perform something. Try to have contrasting speeches to show your range. And never, ever do an accent that you cannot master – it is very embarrassing watching an actor who cannot do the accent required, and you won't be doing yourself any favours.

Don't get disheartened if you don't get the job, it may be due to a number of factors – perhaps you are too tall, or too short, or the wrong age – so never take it personally. Believe in yourself and others will believe in you.'

Rebecca Callard played 'Arietty' in the children's television serial *The Borrowers* when she was 17, and 'Juliet' in Judi Dench's production of *Romeo and Juliet* for the New Shakespeare Company at the Regent's Park Open Air Theatre. She has since graduated to adult roles, playing 'Kate' in the Granada Television serial *The Grand*, for which she was nominated for two 'Best Actress Awards', and the tour representative 'Laura' in the BBC Television series *Sunburn* set in Cyprus and later in Portugal. She recently returned to the New Shakespeare Company to play 'Hermia' in *A Midsummer Night's Dream*.

'I've always wanted to be an actress, ever since I can remember. It's in my blood, I think. I fell into it when I was young, and now I look back I can't believe how lucky I was. It was so easy to get an Equity card back then and before I knew it I was going from job to job.

When you're young you don't get nerves because it's not the end of the world if you don't get a job. But as you get older there seem to be more and more talented actresses and less and less work. I've been fortunate enough to be pretty much constantly working. I don't know why or how, I really think it is just luck. I can't remember ever having a bad audition or being truly nervous before I was 18. But then, once I started to want jobs so badly, I'd have to concentrate on keeping control and focusing. At 19, 20 I still looked 15 so when I auditioned for parts of my own age invariably it didn't work out. Which knocks your confidence. But then as you get older you realise there are all sorts of reasons why you might get rejected. (And it really does seem like rejection.) You might be too small, too tall, too blonde or too brunette or even too young-looking! All these things can make you feel like a failure. But you're not, and you must turn those feelings around and become stronger. It really can be something about your appearance that stops you getting a job. So I believe that you must do one hundred percent the best audition you can do, and then if you don't get it you can't blame yourself.

If I get pages or a script for television or film early enough, I will learn the lines. They tend to tape most auditions now so looking down at the page won't show your face or eyes. Obviously if you get the script just before you go in, go through it as many times as you can.

With theatre I first read the whole play, and then read the scenes out loud over and over again until I'm familiar enough with the lines to be ready to move them around if the director wants to. I work really hard on auditions and lock myself away for days. If I don't get the part I've conditioned myself to move on to the next. And at least I know I worked as hard as I could.

I look at it this way: if I'm out of work, auditions are my only chance to act. And that's all I can do, really!'

A Word About The Speeches

Each of the following speeches has its own introduction, giving the date of the original production – information often required for auditions and drama examinations – a few lines about the play itself and the scene leading up to the actual speech. Even so, it is important to read the *whole* play. Not only are you likely to be asked questions, such as 'What happened in the previous scene?', but the other characters in the play can also give you vital information about your own character.

At the top left corner of each introduction I have – where possible – given the age or approximate age of the character, together with their nationality and/or the region or area they come from. If a region or nationality is not mentioned then standard English, RP (Received Pronunciation) or your own normal voice should be used.

Some characters, such as Frankie in *Member of the Wedding* and Carl in *Madame Melville* are very young. But these are leading parts and are played on stage by older and more experienced actors, usually in their early twenties. They are, however, excellent speeches for young actors and students in the '16 plus' group as well as even younger actors for both auditions and drama examinations.

CHOOSING A SPEECH
Make sure you read audition requirements carefully, particularly with regard to your classical speech. The classical speeches in this book are from plays written in the following periods:

Elizabethan (1558–1603)
Romeo and Juliet and *A Midsummer Night's Dream*
Jacobean (1603–1625)
The Witch of Edmonton
Late Eighteenth Century
The Rivals and *She Stoops To Conquer*
Late Nineteenth Century
An Ideal Husband
Early Twentieth Century
Fanny's First Play and *Back to Methuselah*

SHAKESPEARE'S PLAYS

The speeches used here from *A Midsummer Night's Dream* and *Romeo and Juliet* are all written in blank verse. A speech from Shakespeare or another Elizabethan/Jacobean play is usually one of the requirements for auditioning for full-time drama school, and also for drama exams at the Guildhall School of Music and Drama and the London Academy of Music and Drama (LAMDA).

Professional theatre companies like the Royal Shakespeare, the Royal National Theatre, the New Shakespeare Company at Regent's Park, the marvellous London Bubble Theatre and the various Open Air Theatre companies producing Shakespeare up and down the country also expect you to be able to cope with blank verse.

So it can be a useful source of work for those that take the trouble to learn to do it well!

Blank verse is verse that does not rhyme, but has a recognisable rhythm. Fortunately, the rhythm used by Shakespeare and by most playwrights in this period is the one we use now in everyday speech. It is the measure, pulse or pattern most natural to the English Language: an unstressed syllable followed by stressed syllable. When actors understand this, they find speaking blank verse very much easier than they thought, and realise they don't need to declaim it in tortured tones or stand up and recite it like a poem. These speeches come from plays, and plays are meant to be acted.

There are many instances in blank verse where there is no punctuation at the end of a line and you need to read straight on to the next line to make the speech make sense. For example, in Juliet's speech from *Romeo and Juliet*, the lines:

> Now is the sun upon the highmost hill
> Of this day's journey, and from nine to twelve
> Is three long hours, yet she is not come . . .

If you take a great breath after 'highmost hill' and again after 'twelve' the speech will be choppy and will not make good sense. Similarly Romeo's speech:

> More honourable state, more courtship lives
> In carrion flies than Romeo. They may seize
> On the white wonder of dear Juliet's hand
> And steal immortal blessing from her lips . . .

A breath taken after 'lives' and 'seize' would spoil both the sense and the language and it would not be easily understood.

Most people agree that you should not take a breath at the end of a line where the sense runs on, but there are of course exceptions to this rule – depending sometimes on a particular characterisation or mood, and often in a production, or the Director's own ideas on the subject. But at an audition or drama examination I think it's best to be on the safe side!

Valerie King BA (Hons) Cert Ed, LLAM (Hons), LGSM; Head of Drama at Laine Theatre Arts and Examiner for the London Academy of Music and Dramatic Art (LAMDA) has this to say:

'The author's eclectic choice of stimulating and challenging scenes will surely inspire young performers.

Jean Marlow presents a range of literature from different periods and cultures. These scenes are varied in subject, tone, mood, language and style. The useful introductions help to set the scene in context and provide valuable background information.

These innovative and carefully researched scenes are eminently suitable for auditions, examinations and festivals, enabling young actors to present a broad and balanced programme well suited to their artistic capabilities and talents.'

Audition Speeches for Men

Valentine
(Aged 16)

After Juliet

Sharman Macdonald

This is a BT National Connections project presented as part of the
Celebration of Youth Theatre. It was first performed in the summer
of 1999 at the Royal National Theatre by Cardiff High School and
Strode's College Theatre Company on the Cottesloe and Olivier
stages.

After the tragic deaths of Romeo and Juliet an uneasy truce exists
between the Montague and Capulet families. Benvolio, Romeo's
best friend, is in love with Rosaline, Juliet's cousin. However
Rosaline still loves Romeo and is bent on revenge.

In this scene it is raining. Rosaline enters holding a single lily,
which she throws onto a pile of lilies in the corner of the piazza as
she speaks angrily to the dead Juliet. Benvolio and VALENTINE,
twin brother of Mercutio who was killed trying to defend Romeo,
watch her from the shadows. VALENTINE warns Benvolio to leave
Rosaline alone.

From: *Connections Series*
Published by Faber & Faber, London

VALENTINE

Jealous of dead Juliet.
Oh Lord. Oh Lord.
These Capulets.
Love?
This is love.
A pile of rotting lilies . . .
A pile of stinking lilies bathed in catpiss,
Only you would see the fresh ones on the top.
And love Rosaline whose heart's in the grave.
There are softer beds to lie on
Than fair Rosaline's nail strewn cot . . .
She'd have you for breakfast.
That girl is the enemy.
She'd eat you up, suck on the bits
And after, lick her chops.
She's a hurt animal.
A cat that would attack the hand
That gentles it.
And bite it hard.
Princess of Cats.
She's a better man
Than Tybalt ever was
Or Petruchio ever shall be.
Give her a sword
She'd show you no mercy.
Though she has no need of a sword.
What woman does?
While the Prince has taken our weapons
He's left them theirs . . .
Have you no sisters?
A woman's weapon is her tongue.
See her. See.
Conjoin with her.
You'll fight the oldest feud of all.
Not Montagues and Capulets.
Men and women Benvolio.
Men and women. There's a war.
Will never end by any decree
Of man, or Prince, or God. Don't go near her.

Wint Selby
(American – aged 19)

Ah! Wilderness

Eugene O'Neill

First performed at the Nixon Theatre, Pittsburgh, Pennsylvania, in 1933 and transferred in the same year to the Guild Theatre, New York. It is a comedy set in 1906 and described as a study of middle-class family life.

Nat Miller, owner of *The Evening Globe*, lives in Connecticut with his wife and four children – Arthur, the eldest who is at Yale, 16-year-old Richard, and young Mildred and Tommy. It is the Fourth of July and the family are at dinner. Richard's girlfriend has left him and he is feeling wretched. His mother tells him it is his own fault. Upset, he walks out of the dining room.

Outside he hears a low whistle coming from the porch. It is WINT SELBY, a classmate of Arthur's at Yale and a typical college boy of the period. He has called to see Arthur but he is out. He explains to Richard that he has dated a couple of girls for the night, but cannot afford to buy drinks for both of them. The situation is urgent. Richard offers to lend him 11 dollars. But WINT doesn't want his money, he wants Richard to stand in for his elder brother.

Published by Jonathan Cape, London

WINT

(*As he enters - warningly, in a low tone*) Keep it quiet, Kid. I don't want the folks to know I'm here. Tell Art I want to see him a second – on the QT . . . (*irritably*) Damn! I thought he'd be here for dinner. (*More irritably*) Hell, that gums the works for fair! . . . I ran into a couple of swift babies from New Haven this after, and I dated them up for tonight, thinking I could catch Art. But now it's too late to get anyone else and I'll have to pass it up. I'm nearly broke and I can't afford to blow them both to drinks . . . (*shaking his head*) Nix, Kid, I don't want to borrow your money. (*Then getting an idea*) But say, have you got anything on for tonight?. . . Want to come along with me? (*Then quickly*) I'm not trying to lead you astray, understand. But it'll be a help if you would just sit around with Belle and feed her a few drinks while I'm off with Edith. (*He winks*) See what I mean? You don't have to do anything, not even take a glass of beer – unless you want to . . . Ever been out with any girls– I mean, real swift ones that there's something doing with, not these dead Janes around here . . . Ever drink anything besides sodas? . . . (*impressed*) Hell, you know more than I thought. (*Then considering*) Can you fix it so your folks won't get wise? I don't want your old man coming after me. You can get back by half-past ten or eleven, though, all right. Think you can cook up some lie to cover that? (*As RICHARD hesitates – encouraging him*) Ought to be easy – on the Fourth . . . But you've got to keep your face closed about this, you hear? – to Art and everybody else. I tell you straight, I wouldn't ask you to come if I wasn't in a hole – and if I didn't know you were coming down to Yale next year, and didn't think you're giving me the straight goods about having been around before. I don't want to lead you astray . . . Well, you be at the Pleasant Beach Hotel at half-past nine then. Come in the back room. And don't forget to grab some cloves to take the booze off your breath . . . See you later, then. (*He starts out and is just about to close the door when he thinks of something*) And say, I'll say you're a Harvard freshman, and you back me up. They don't know a damn thing about Harvard. I don't want them thinking I'm travelling around with any high-school kid . . . So long then. You better beat it right after your dinner while you've got a chance, and hang around until it's time. Watch your step, Kid.

Guy Bennett
(Aged 17)

Another Country
Julian Mitchell

First produced at the Greenwich Theatre in 1981, then transferred to the Queens Theatre, London, and revived at The Arts Theatre, London, in 2000.

The play takes place in an English public school in the early 30s, where future leaders of the ruling class are being prepared for their entry into the Establishment. In this environment the two central characters – GUY BENNETT, coming to terms with his homosexuality, and Tommy Judd, a committed Marxist – are very much 'outsiders'.

In this scene, set in the fourth-year library, BENNETT, Judd and Devenish are talking about the Dedication they have just attended. Judd dismisses it as ludicrous for 400 boys to line up and blub for a lot of people they never knew who died in a businessman's war. BENNETT remarks that it made him think of his father whom he loathed, and goes on to describe in detail the ghastly circumstances of his death.

Published by Amber Lane Press

BENNETT

It was the Easter hols. I was reading in bed one night when I heard the most peculiar noise – a sort of muffled squeaking. I thought it was the cat at first. But then it went on and on – sort of feeble and desperate at the same time. Like something trapped. So I got up and looked out into the passage. It seemed to be coming from my parents' room, and there was a light under the door, so I assumed – well, I mean, what would you have thought? . . . I was just going back to bed to mind my own business, and feeling pretty queasy because – well, I mean, one's own parents! . . . When I quite distinctly heard my mater say, 'Help!' (*He imitates her*) 'Help!' (DEVENISH *is enthralled.* JUDD *is more and more sceptical*) It was terribly eerie. Complete silence, then suddenly there it was again. 'Help!' So – I didn't know what to do. I went down the passage to their door. I listened a moment, then I knocked and said, 'Are you all right?' And she said – (*Imitation of the muffled voice again*) – 'Guy! Quick – help!' She sounded absolutely at her last gasp. So I turned the door handle to go in – only of course the door was locked . . . All the bedroom keys are the same in our house. I see why now. But it took me ages to push their key out backwards and get mine in. And then, when I finally got the door open – my pater had had a heart attack right in the middle of – (JUDD *claps ironically,* BENNETT *turns on him*) Have you ever tried lifting your father's corpse off your living mother? . . . It's incredibly difficult. He was like a huge sack of – of wet mud. The weight never went where I was expecting . . . My mother kept her eyes shut the whole time. I suppose she thought if she couldn't see me, I couldn't see her. But of course I could . . . He was a very fleshy man. And they were in rather a complicated position. I think that's what did it. The mechanics were too much for him. There was a ghastly moment I thought I might have to break one of his arms . . . What made it all the more macabre was, I'd always hated him. He was a complete loather. Whereas my mother – I couldn't help thinking – it's all right for him – what better way to go? But for *her* – and *me*, seeing her, like it says in the Bible, uncovered – I honestly wondered if we'd ever be able to look each other in the eye again. If you ask me, it's why she's marrying this awful Colonel person.

Morgan Evans
(Welsh – aged 17)

The Corn is Green

Emlyn Williams

First produced at the Duchess Theatre, London, in 1938 and set in a mining village in the Welsh countryside in the late 1800s.

An English teacher, Miss Moffat, comes down from London to take over the house left to her by her uncle. There is an old barn next door and she decides to turn it into a school for the local children. One of her pupils – a young miner, MORGAN EVANS – shows exceptional promise and for the next two years she takes a special interest in him, eventually persuading the local squire to fund his application for a scholarship to Oxford.

In this scene MORGAN has begun to resent his studies and, unknown to Miss Moffat, has been drinking every evening in the Gwesmor Arms with the local lads. Miss Moffat tells him she has entered him for the scholarship and is going to start teaching him Greek. She has also found him a nail-file and will show him how to use it. MORGAN flings his pen down on the table and announces that he is going back to the coal-mine.

Published by Heinemann Educational Books, Oxford

MORGAN

(*Quietly*) I shall not need a nail-file in the coal-mine . . . I am going back to the coal-mine . . . (*She turns and looks at him. He rises, breathing fast. They look at each other. A pause*) I do not want to learn Greek, nor to pronounce any long English words, nor to keep my hands clean . . . Because . . . (*plunging*) . . . because I was born in a Welsh hayfield when my mother was helpin' with the harvest – and I always lived in a little house with no stairs only a ladder – and no water – and until my brothers was killed I never sleep except three in a bed. I know that is terrible grammar but it is true . . . The last two years I have not had no proper talk with English chaps in the mine because I was so busy keepin' this old grammar in its place. Tryin' to better myself . . . (*his voice rising*) . . . tryin' to better myself, the day and the night! . . . You cannot take a nail-file into the Gwesmor Arms public bar! . . . I have been there every afternoon for a week, spendin' your pocket-money, and I have been there now, and that is why I can speak my mind! . . . Because you are not interested in me . . . (*losing control*) How can you be interested in a machine that you put a penny in and if nothing comes out you give it a good shake? 'Evans, write me an essay, Evans, get up and bow, Evans, what is a subjunctive!' My name is Morgan Evans, and all my friends call me Morgan, and if there is anything gets on the wrong side of me it is callin' me Evans! . . . And do you know what they call me in the village? Ci bach yr ysgol! The schoolmistress's little dog. What has it got to do with you if my nails are dirty? Mind your own business! (*He bursts into sobs and buries his head in his hands on the end of the sofa.*)

Honey
(Aged 18)

Cressida

Nicholas Wright

First produced by the Almeida Theatre at the Albery Theatre, London, in March 2000.

Actor and talent scout John Shank is a trainer of boy players in the London theatre of the 1630s. He has foolishly invested in Master Gunnell's theatre, but Gunnell has disappeared and Shank is on the edge of financial ruin. Before he left, Gunnell sent him a new boy, Stephen Hammerton, who begged Shank to train him as an actor, but now it seems he will have to be sold.

It is late at night and Stephen, together with an older boy, HONEY, has crept through the trap door into the costume store of Master Gunnell's theatre. It appears to be stripped bare, but behind the curtains are some expensive gowns. If they can take these back to Shank he can pay off his debts and Stephen won't have to be sold after all.

In this scene HONEY has tried on one of the gowns and is smoking a pipe. Stephen has always admired HONEY, who is extremely experienced and one of Shank's most talented and successful young players. Stephen asks him to explain about acting. Is it all just 'a matter of standing straight and saying your lines'?

(*'Jhon' – an old theatre dresser at the Globe*)

Published by Nick Hern Books, London

HONEY

It's different at different times . . . When you're young, you're just a child being clever. Then it changes . . . When you get older. When other boys get tall and clumsy. And their voices drop two million pegs. We don't do that. We hang on . . . It's like a baby falling down a well. You've got its foot in your hand and you don't let go. So you're not one thing exactly. You're half man, half boy. That's when you find you can really do it. And it's amazing. It's better than beer or wine. It's better than smoking. It's like flying. It's like finding that wings have suddenly sprouted from your shoulders. You come on stage and everything happens the way it's meant to. And nobody in the audience looks at anyone else. Because you live in a sort of stolen time that they can't get to. Except through you. And it could disappear at any moment. You're like a soldier on the eve of battle. Every night could be your last. And everyone wants to be that special person on that special night. That's my theory. That's why they grab old Jhon, J, H, O, N, and give him notes for us. It's why they hang about at the Actors' Door. (*He puts out the pipe, starts getting out of his dress*) I still get letters every day. Not just from men. Everyone thinks I'm just a boyish bugger. That's not true. I see women as well. They're even stranger than the men are. They ask me to supper and want me to bring my gown and make-up. (*He stands, the gown in his arms*) Take it. (STEPHEN *takes it*. HONEY *gets the other gowns*) We'll carry them back to Shanky. He'll pay his debt to the Board and you'll stay on. Isn't that what you wanted?

Billy
(West of Ireland – aged 17–18)

The Cripple of Inishmaan

Martin McDonagh

First performed at the Cottesloe auditorium of the Royal National Theatre in 1996 and set on a remote island off the west coast of Ireland in 1934.

A Hollywood film director has arrived on the neighbouring Island of Inishmore to film *Man of Aran* and young cripple BILLY is determined to get a part. Pretending to have contracted TB, he produces a supposed letter from the doctor saying he hasn't much longer to live and persuades local fisherman Babbybobby, whose wife had recently died of the disease, to take him across to Inishmore on his boat. There is a part for a cripple boy in the film and BILLY is taken to Hollywood to test for the role. The test turns out to be a complete failure and BILLY returns to Inishmaan, shamed by his experience.

In this scene he apologises to Bobbybabby for 'codding' him along and attempts to explain what has happened. Bobby's reply is to pick up a length of lead piping and knock him to the ground.

Published by Methuen Drama

BILLY

Babbybobby. I daresay I owe you an explanation . . . I want to, Bobby. See, I never thought at all this day would come when I'd have to explain. I'd hoped I'd disappear forever to America. And I would've too, if they'd wanted me there. If they'd wanted me for the filming. But they didn't want me. A blond lad from Fort Lauderdale they hired instead of me. He wasn't crippled at all, but the Yank said, 'Ah, better to get a normal fella who can act crippled than a crippled fella who can't fecking act at all.' Except he said it ruder. (*Pause*) I thought I'd done alright for meself with me acting. Hours I practised in me hotel there. And all for nothing. (*Pause*) I gave it a go anyways. I had to give it a go. I had to get away from this place, Babbybobby, be any means, just like me mammy and daddy had to get away from this place. (*Pause*) Going drowning meself I'd often think of when I was here, just to . . . just to end the laughing at me, and the sniping at me, and the life of nothing but shuffling to the doctor's and shuffling back from the doctor's and pawing over the same oul books and finding any other way to piss another day away. Another day of sniggering, or the patting me on the head like a broken-brained gosawer. The village orphan. The village cripple, and nothing more. Well, there are plenty round here just as crippled as me, only it isn't on the outside it shows. (*Pause*) But the thing is, you're not one of them, Babbybobby, nor never were. You've a kind heart on you. I suppose that's why it was so easy to cod you with the TB letter, but that's why I was so sorry for codding you at the time and why I'm just as sorry now. Especially for codding you with the same thing your Mrs passed from. Just I thought that would be more effective. But in the long run, I thought, or I hoped, that if you had a choice between you being codded a while and me doing away with meself, once your anger had died down anyways, you'd choose you being codded every time. Was I wrong, Babbybobby? Was I?

Sloane
(Young)

Entertaining Mr Sloane

Joe Orton

This black comedy was first produced at Wyndham's Theatre, London, in 1964 and more recently at The Arts Theatre, London, in 2001.

Mr SLOANE is a young psychopath, ruthless and single-minded. When he arrives at landlady Kath's house looking for a room, she and her brother, Ed, welcome him with open arms. He is such a nice young man and both are intent on seducing him. Only their elderly father, Kemp, is suspicious of SLOANE, having seen him somewhere before. SLOANE silences him by kicking him to death. Brother and sister now have SLOANE exactly where they want him and each agree to 'share' him for six months of the year.

In this scene SLOANE is alone with Kemp. He pulls the old man's stick away from him, pushes him into a chair and demands to know what he has been saying about him. Kemp foolishly accuses him of killing his 'old boss'.

From: *Orton, The Complete Plays – Master Playwrights*
Published by Methuen Drama

SLOANE

Your vision is faulty. You couldn't identify nobody now. So long after. You said so yourself . . . Sit still! (*Silence*) . . . It was an accident, Pop. I'm innocent. You don't know the circumstances . . . Accidental death . . . You're pre-judging my case . . . Keep quiet. (*Silence*) It's like this see. One day I leave the Home. Stroll along. Sky blue. Fresh air. They'd found me a likeable permanent situation. Canteen facilities. Fortnight's paid holiday. Overtime? Time and a half after midnight. A staff dance each year. What more could one wish to devote one's life to? I certainly loved that place. The air round Twickenham was like wine. Then one day I take a trip to the old man's grave. Hic Jacets in profusion. Ashes to Ashes. Alas the fleeting. The sun was declining. A few press-ups on a tomb belonging to a family name of Cavaneagh, and I left the graveyard. I thumbs a lift from a geyser who promises me a bed. Gives me a bath. And a meal. Very friendly. All you could wish he was, a photographer. He shows me one or two experimental studies. An experience for the retina and no mistake. He wanted to photo me. For certain interesting features I had that he wanted the exclusive right of preserving. You know how it is. I didn't like to refuse. No harm in it I suppose. But then I got to thinking . . . I knew a kid once called MacBride that happened to. Oh, yes . . . so when I gets to think of this I decide I got to do something about it. And I gets up in the middle of the night looking for the film see. He has a lot of expensive equipment about in his studio see. Well it appears that he gets the wrong idea. Runs in. Gives a shout. And the long and the short of it is I loses my head which is a thing I never ought to a done with the worry of them photos an all. And I hits him. I hits him. (*Pause*) He must have had a weak heart. Something like that I should imagine. Definitely should have seen his doctor before that. I wasn't to know was I? I'm not to blame. (*Silence*)

Steve
(Aged 20)

Flatmates

Ellen Dryden

First workshopped and performed by the Chiswick Youth Theatre and published in 2000, the action takes place in a student flat in the 1990s.

STEVE, a law student whose wealthy parents own the flat, lets out two rooms to Lynn and Tom, who are studying English.

In this opening scene, STEVE is sitting at an old wooden dining table loaded with milk bottles, cartons and cornflake packets consuming a large breakfast. Lynn sits opposite him removing her nail varnish. They are both in a disagreeable mood. Tom joins them. He has been sitting up most of the night writing an essay and is not at his best. STEVE has taken his milk and poured it into his coffee – they quarrel and Tom finally rushes out of the room. STEVE comments that Tom is getting tiresome. Lynn starts to collect up her things. This is worse than sharing with her girlfriends Kate and Abbey: at least they only rowed about fellas. 'Wheels within undercurrents' are more than she can take.

From: *Six Primroses Each and other Plays for Young Actors*
Published by First Writes Publications, London

STEVE

What a command of metaphor you do have, my dear Lynn. Strikes me all you English lot have got too much time on your hands and not enough intellectual meat . . .What was that you wrote – when you last wrote an essay that is – all that junk about the 'closely woven texture' of George Eliot's prose? Closely woven cerrap! It's unhealthy, all this poring over literature. Makes you think you've got feelings. You all need a dose of nice, detached, unemotional law . . . (*Pushing away his plate*) Now. What shall I have for lunch? There's a rather piquant little terrine of crab I've had my eye on for a while. But do I feel fishy today? And would Tom cast it in my face in a rage thinking I'd been at his tinned pilchards? . . . If he must work so hard to please that rancid little mouse of a mother of his, that's his problem . . . She believes Tom is the sun, the moon and the stars . . . A bloodsucker. Keeping poor old Tom scribbling little pictures labelled 'Mummy' and writing pathetic letters from 'your loving little son'. It's time he shoved her under a bus and went out and did something outrageous like going on the Tube without paying! Much better to have a mother like mine. She can just about remember who I am when I'm actually there. She lost interest in me when I stopped being a curly headed little accessory to her fashion photos . . . Tom's wound up so tight there'll be bits found all over the Home Counties when he finally splits! . . . Get out of the way! Don't be self-indulgent, Lynn. All you're really bothered about is a good time – so don't pretend to be all caring and compassionate about Tom. It's nauseating. Mummy'll come and pick up the pieces and put them in a plastic bag and take them home and stick them all together again. (*Pause*) I'm thinking of asking Tom to leave, actually . . . He's only paying me half of what you do, you know. Why should I subsidise Tom because I've had the forethought to have a rich Mummy and Daddy who look after me instead of a whinging little apology of a female who managed to get herself pregnant at fifteen and didn't do anything about it. I think it's unhealthy to have a mother who's only a few years older than you. And who was his Dad? Some visually handicapped passer-by? . . . never promise to keep secrets, Lynn dear. Much too exhausting.

Tom
(American – young)

The Glass Menagerie

Tennessee Williams

First performed in London at the Theatre Royal, Haymarket, in 1948 and set in the Wingfield family apartment in a tenement building in St Louis, *The Glass Menagerie* is described as a 'memory' play.

TOM WINGFIELD recalls his life in St Louis with his mother, Amanda, and his crippled sister Laura. Amanda clings to the past and her memories of the 'gentlemen callers' who were once so numerous. Laura lives in a world of her own among her collection of glass animals. Meanwhile, TOM himself spends all his spare time in the cinema in order to escape the intolerable situation at home. When he arrives home with his friend Jim, Amanda welcomes the visitor as a potential 'gentleman caller' for her daughter. But although Jim is kind and sympathetic towards Laura he is already engaged to another girl. Amanda blames TOM for her daughter's disappointment, accusing him of having known about his friend's engagement before bringing him home.

In this earlier scene, TOM is quarrelling with his mother. She has confiscated his books as she considers them unsuitable and tells him she is 'at the end of her patience'.

Published by Penguin Books, London

TOM

What do you think I'm at? Aren't I supposed to have any patience to reach the end of, Mother? I know, I know. It seems unimportant to you, what I'm *doing* – what I *want* to do – having a little *difference* between them! . . . Listen! You think I'm crazy about the *warehouse*? (*He bends fiercely toward her slight figure*) You think I'm in love with the Continental Shoemakers? You think I want to spend fifty-five *years* down there in that – *celotex interior*! with – *fluorescent* – *tubes*! Look! I'd rather somebody picked up a crowbar and battered out my brains – than go back mornings! I *go*! Every time you come in yelling that God damn *'Rise and Shine!' 'Rise and Shine!'* I say to myself, 'How *lucky dead* people are!' But I get up. *I go*! For sixty-five dollars a month I give up all that I dream of doing and being *ever*! And you say self – *self's* all I ever think of. Why, listen, if self is what I thought of, Mother, I'd be where he is – GONE! (*Pointing to father's picture*) As far as the system of transportation reaches! (*He starts past her. She grabs his arm*) Don't grab at me, Mother! . . . I'm going to the *movies*! . . . (*Crouching towards her, overtowering her tiny figure. She backs away, gasping*) I'm going to opium dens! Yes, opium dens, dens of vice and criminals' hang-outs, Mother. I've joined the Hogan gang, I'm a hired assassin, I carry a tommy-gun in a violin case! I run a string of cat-houses in the Valley! The call me Killer, Killer Wingfield, I'm leading a double-life, a simple, honest warehouse worker by day, by night a dynamic *tsar of the underworld*, *Mother*. I go to gambling casinos, I spin away fortunes on the roulette table! I wear a patch over one eye and a false moustache, sometimes I put on green whiskers. On those occasions they call me – *El Diablo!* Oh, I could tell you things to make you sleepless! My enemies plan to dynamite this place. They're going to blow us all sky-high some night! I'll be glad, very happy, and so will you! You'll go up, up on a broomstick, over Blue Mountain with seventeen gentlemen callers! You ugly – babbling old – *witch* . . . (*He goes*).

Raleigh
(Aged 18)

Journey's End

R C Sherriff

First produced at the Apollo Theatre in 1928 and set in March 1918 towards the end of the First World War.

The action takes place over three days in a dug-out in France and shows the effect of war on a group of young Officers – some of them not long out of school. SECOND LIEUTENANT RALEIGH has been assigned to Captain Stanhope's Company. He is young and enthusiastic and welcomed by everyone with the exception of Stanhope, who is not at all happy about the new appointment.

In this early scene RALEIGH has just arrived and introduces himself to Osborne, Stanhope's second in command. Osborne offers him a whiskey and asks if he knows Captain Stanhope.

Published by Penguin Books, London

RALEIGH

Yes, rather! We were at school together – at least – of course – I was only a kid and he was one of the big fellows; he's three years older than I am . . . He was skipper of Rugger at Barford, and kept wicket for the eleven. A jolly good bat, too . . . Oh, I think he'll remember me. (*He stops, and goes on rather awkwardly*) You see, it wasn't only that we were just at school together; our fathers were friends, and Dennis used to come and stay with us in the holidays. Of course, at school I didn't see much of him, but in the holidays we were terrific pals . . . Last time he was on leave he came down to the school; he'd just got his MC and been made a captain. He looked splendid! It – sort of – made me feel . . . keen . . . Yes. Keen to get out here. I was frightfully keen to get into Dennis's regiment. I thought, perhaps, with a bit of luck I might get to the same battalion . . . I know. It's an amazing bit of luck. When I was at the base I did an awful thing. You see, my uncle's at the base – he has to detail officers to regiments – General Raleigh. I went to see him on the quiet and asked him if he could get me into this battalion. He bit my head off, and said I'd got to be treated like everybody else – and next day I was told I *was* coming to this battalion. Funny, wasn't it? . . . And when I got to Battalion Headquarters, and the colonel told me to report to 'C' Company, I could have cheered. I expect Dennis'll be frightfully surprised to see me. I've got a message for him. From my sister. You see, Dennis used to stay with us, and naturally my sister (*he hesitates*) – well – perhaps I ought not . . . They're not – er – officially engaged . . . She'll be awfully glad I'm with him here; I can write and tell her all about him. He doesn't say much in his letters; can we write often? (*There is a pause*) You don't think Dennis'll mind my – sort of – forcing myself into his company? I never thought of that; I was so keen.

Harry
(Lancashire – aged 17)

Love on the Dole

Ronald Gow and Walter Greenwood

First performed at the Manchester Repertory Theatre in 1934 and in London at the Garrick Theatre in 1935, *Love on the Dole* is set in Hanky Park, Salford, Lancashire.

In Hanky Park in the 1930s, unemployment is high. Mr Hardcastle is on the dole and his wife takes in washing. Their daughter Sally works in a mill – the only one in the family bringing in a decent wage. Their son, HARRY, earns 17 shillings a week in a machine shop at the local foundry, but already many of his fellow workers have been laid off. He is courting Helen, a 16-year-old local girl, and they are planning to get married. When he wins 22 pounds on the horses it seems like a fortune and he shares it among the family.

In this scene it is a year later and HARRY has lost his job in the machine shop. Mrs Hardcastle is in the kitchen making up a bundle of things to take to the pawnshop when HARRY comes in looking troubled. The Public Assistance Committee have cut his dole money and to make matters worse, Helen is pregnant.

Published by Samuel French, London

HARRY

(*Sits by the table and stares at the floor*) Ma . . . I've got bad news . . . They've knocked me off the dole money . . . They've knocked me off the dole, I tell you . . . It's the Public Assistance Committee. They say the money's got to stop because Sally's working and Dad's getting the dole as it is. They say there's enough coming into one house . . . But – it's Helen I'm thinking of. You see, we were going to get married . . . I mean we've got to! . . . Ay – she's seen the doctor – we've got to . . . Look here, Ma, it isn't that I don't want to marry her. I do. I like her better than – well, anything, and we was planning to marry. We was going to make do on my dole money and what she's getting herself, and now this happens. If only we can get a start. I'll be drawing the dole again as soon as we are wed. And I thought perhaps – Well, I thought you and Dad would let her come here, and we could share the back room with Sally . . . Oh, gosh, Ma, it's driving me barmy. (*He breaks down and buries his face.* MRS HARDCASTLE *turns to* HARRY *and timidly puts her hand on his shoulder*) Sorry, Ma, but I'm ashamed to walk the streets. I feel they're all watching me. I've been to twenty places this morning and it's the same blasted story all the time. 'No hands wanted.' Though they don't usually say it so polite. And look at me clothes. It'll take six months' pay to buy new ones. Aw, God, just let me get a job. I don't care if it's only half-pay, but give me something . . . (HARDCASTLE *comes in from the street, hangs up his cap, looks from one to the other*) You see, Dad, I'll have to marry her and I thought . . . I thought, maybe, that we could come and live here and get a bed in back room with Sal . . . (*rises – warmly*) Hey! I'm not having you calling her a slut. Just you leave her name out of it . . . I'm asking you for nothing. I'm not the only one out of work in this house, remember. Yah, you treat me like a kid just because I've got nothing and I'm out of work. You didn't talk like that when I was sharing my winnings with you, did you? Once let me get hold of some money again and I'll never part with a penny of it. I'm supposed to be a man, I am – Well, look at me. Aye, and if there was another war you'd call me a man too. I'd be a bloody hero then . . . I don't want to live here. Do you understand? I wouldn't live with you if I got the chance. You can go to hell! I'm leaving here.

Carl
(Aged 15)

Madame Melville

Richard Nelson

First performed at the Vaudeville Theatre, London, in October 2000, and set in Paris in 1966.

Madame Melville is the story of CARL, a 15-year-old American boy, and his brief relationship with his literature teacher, the beautiful Claudie Melville.

Claudie invites CARL to join her special students who meet twice a week to see and discuss the latest films. The discussions take place in her apartment over chocolates and cocoa or tea. One evening she persuades him to stay on after the others have left. He misses his last train and she suggests he spend the night with her. She promises to take him to the Louvre the following afternoon.

In this speech, CARL describes their walk along the Quai du Louvre and Claudie's encounter with his mathematics teacher, Monsieur Darc.

Published by Faber & Faber, London

CARL

Outside we walked together along the Quai du Louvre. Mme Melville stopped at a kiosk and purchased a small book of paintings from the museum. I watched her take out her money, bending a leg to hold up the purse. The late-afternoon, early summer's sun seemed to touch her and set her apart from the world. As if a sculpture. As if a work of art.

(*Beat*)

I felt more desire than I'd ever in my life felt before.

(*Beat*)

The book was for me. She brushed back her hair, which the wind off the Seine kept blowing across her face. 'A souvenir,' she explained, as she placed it into my jacket pocket. The expression on my face, I think, stopped her, stopped her smiling. And then for the first time, though we had been together all day, all night, in her apartment, in her bed, I reached and I touched her. I touched her arm, and then held it. And I would have kissed her – until then I had never kissed a girl – but I would have kissed her had she not suddenly run off.

(*Short pause*)

She ran to a man I recognised as Monsieur Darc, my mathematics teacher at school. With him was his young daughter holding a balloon. They kissed each other on the cheeks. They spoke. She seemed to talk very sternly at him. They did not kiss good-bye.

(*Beat*)

Walking home she asked if I wanted to stop for coffee. Then she ordered wine. Suddenly it was like I wasn't even there. She found a pair of sunglasses in her bag and put them on. We sat there for a long time. And then we returned to her apartment.

George
(Liverpool – aged 17)

Presence

David Harrower

First presented at the Royal Court Jerwood Theatre Upstairs in 2001 and set in Hamburg.

It is 1960 and memories of an horrific past – a Nazi Germany and a city ablaze where human fat once ran in the gutters – still persist.

A group of three lads from Liverpool, GEORGE, Pete and Paul, have been hired to play in the run-down Indra Club for six weeks. Their accommodation consists of a dingy basement room with two beds and a sofa. Pete and Paul have claimed the two beds. GEORGE, the youngest, has had to sleep on the sofa.

In this scene it is mid-morning. GEORGE is standing by the wall trying to write a card home to his parents. On the front of the card is a picture of Hamburg. He holds it up to read the inscription to the others, then returns to the sofa.

Published by Faber & Faber, London

GEORGE

What'm I supposed to write on this stupid thing? Eh? . . . (*Holds it up. Reads from back*) 'The historic port of Hamburg sits on the banks of the majestic River Elbe. The whole area pictured was destroyed in the Great Fire of 1842. Maybe that's why our women are so red-hot . . .' I *wouldn't* change places with anyone in the world right now . . . Couple of months here and back in time to do me electrical exams, eh? . . . Listen, it's a solid trade. I know things you don't. Look around this room, you can't see anything. When I look around it, I see it with electrician's eyes . . . It's a deathtrap in here. You don't have a clue. The state of that wiring . . . That's a fire wanting to happen. Not waiting to happen, wanting to happen. Nine times out of ten fire starts when people are sleeping. Almost like it listens till we're off our guard. Judging the right moment to strike. The body unaware. I love fire. Always have. An electrician always knows it's there, over his shoulder, behind everything he does. Saw a charred body once. Went with me brothers – they're both electricians – to a house that'd burnt down. This bloke was sitting on the floor grinning. I wasn't supposed to see him. Looked like he'd enjoyed it happening to him. That was the best thing I ever saw, I think. He was there but he was gone. No eyes, no ears, no insides – they all liquify. His lips had burnt off. He's sitting there, grinning. Petrified . . . Petrified forest. That's what the house looked like. And how d'you think they get him out of there? They'd have had to snap his . . . Like charcoal . . . Just warning you . . . Gives me one over you, doesn't it? When you wake up in the night and me bed's empty . . . (*Pete stands up*) He's smart. He's getting out.

Danny
(Aged 18)

The Present

Nick Ward

First performed at the Bush Theatre, London, in 1995 and set in Melbourne, Australia, in the early 1980s.

DANNY was born in Melbourne but has lived in England since a child. Now he has returned to his birthplace, but things have not gone well for him. He is discovered sleeping rough in a street in Central Melbourne by Michael, an art dealer. Michael invites him home and offers him a job selling paintings. DANNY is told to memorise the life and background of one of the painters, Luke Murray, and then go out and sell the pictures as the painter himself.

DANNY has been invited to supper by an old friend, Libby, but when he arrives Libby is out and he is entertained instead by her flatmate, Becky. Becky is smoking a joint as she supposedly prepares supper while changing into a flimsy black outfit. Embarrassed by her sexual advances, he attempts to leave and she lunges at him with the carving knife.

In this scene it is dawn the following morning. DANNY is alone rehearsing the sales pitch for his first assignment. His ear is bandaged from his encounter with Becky the night before and he has a portfolio of pictures under his arm.

Note: This speech is edited only for reasons of space and in its entirety may be a little long for drama school auditions. However, the whole speech needs to be studied along with the play itself.

Published by Faber & Faber, London

DANNY

(*Monologue*) Good evening. My name is Luke Murray. I'm an artist from England. I'm in Australia on a scholarship from the Royal College of Art in London. I've spent the last few months exploring your Outback and attempting to convey its mysteries in my landscapes. I was wondering whether you might be able to spare me a few minutes to show you my work. (*He moves forward and spreads the paintings out on the floor*) This one? I had a feeling you'd like that one. It's a ghost town called Kookynie in WA. It's my favourite too. There's a bit of a story behind it, actually. I was in Kalgoorlie, low on cash and inspiration. I used to play pool at a run-down hotel in Hay Street. There was a man there that I'll never forget. He had long hair, he was scruffy-looking and wore an old bush hat . . . We shot pool for an afternoon, and again the following day – but we still hadn't exchanged a word. Suddenly, he broke off from the game and made a phone call. I heard him say, 'Libby. It's me. Don't hang up, Libby. I'm in Kalgoorlie, I can't live without you . . .' Down went the phone. He phoned again, but the line was dead. He slumped down in the corner and beckoned to me. I sat down on the floor with him and he told me the story. It's an old, old story, but he told it with such feeling that he made it new. He told me about this woman back in Melbourne. How she'd loved him to the point of madness and how he'd treated her badly. You know, the whole lot: violence, lies, other women, and something about a lost child. But, however badly he treated her, she kept returning. It went on for years, until one day, she woke up and realized that he was killing her. So she left him. It was only then, he told me, when she wasn't there any more, that he was really able to *see* her. But it was too late, because she'd gone and he'd lost her . . . Anyway, that's the story. It's a painting about lost love and the end of a journey . . . What? Well, I'm sure you'll agree that given the fact that it's so important to me, I'm sure you'll understand that I can't really ask for less than . . . one hundred and twenty dollars . . . One hundred . . . ? Let's call it ninety-five – it means a lot to me, you're killing me here . . . OK, ninety . . . eighty-five, I can't go a cent lower . . . For you, madam, yes. Eighty. Eighty bucks. We have a deal . . . (*With a seductive smile*) Thank you. (*He removes the bandage*)

Romeo
(Young)

Romeo and Juliet

William Shakespeare

A tragedy written in or around 1595, and set in Verona, it is the story of two 'star-crossed lovers', ROMEO MONTAGUE and Juliet Capulet, whose tragic deaths end their families' long-standing feud.

ROMEO and Juliet meet and fall in love at a feast given by Juliet's father. The hatred between the Montagues and the Capulets makes it impossible for them to be together and so ROMEO persuades Friar Lawrence to marry them secretly. After the ceremony ROMEO is confronted by Juliet's cousin, Tybalt, who challenges him to a duel. ROMEO refuses to fight, but his friend, Mercutio, takes up the challenge and is killed under ROMEO's arm as he tries to separate them. In fury ROMEO fights and kills Tybalt, then, persuaded by his companions, runs from the scene.

ROMEO is hiding out in the Friar's cell, when the Friar arrives bringing good news. The Duke has not imposed the expected death sentence, but instead has sentenced ROMEO to banishment. He must leave Verona and Juliet.

Published by Penguin Books, London

ROMEO

'Tis torture, and not mercy. Heaven is here,
Where Juliet lives. And every cat and dog
And little mouse, every unworthy thing,
Live here in heaven and may look on her.
But Romeo may not. More validity,
More honourable state, more courtship lives
In carrion flies than Romeo. They may seize
On the white wonder of dear Juliet's hand
And steal immortal blessing from her lips,
Who, even in pure and vestal modesty,
Still blush, as thinking their own kisses sin.
This may flies do, when I from this must fly.
And sayest thou yet that exile is not death?
But Romeo may not, he is banishèd.
Flies may do this but I from this must fly.
They are free men. But I am banishèd.
Hadst thou no poison mixed, no sharp-ground knife,
No sudden mean of death, though ne'er so mean,
But 'banishèd' to kill me – 'banishèd'?
O' Friar, the damnèd use that word in hell.
Howling attends it! How hast thou the heart,
Being a divine, a ghostly confessor,
A sin-absolver, and my friend professed,
To mangle me with that word 'banishèd'?

Lee
(Aged 15)

School Play

Suzy Almond

First produced at the Soho Theatre, London, in 2001.

Charlie Silver is bad news in her South London comprehensive school: a problem to teachers and a bad influence on the rest of the class. Her ambitions are to front a gang, ride a motorbike and to 'mess with teachers' heads'. She boasts a long list of teachers who have given up on her account. Then Miss Fry, the new music teacher, arrives and things begin to change. Charlie is given countless detentions, but unknown to her 'gang' – LEE COULSON who has recently been suspended from school, and his friend Paul – is using these detention periods to develop her suppressed musical talents.

In this scene, Charlie is at the piano waiting for Miss Fry to arrive when LEE comes bursting in. He accuses her of letting him down. She was supposed to meet him and Paul in the car park earlier that afternoon with her customised Hollister bike on which he was to ride 'a lap of honour' against his rival, Danny Chapel. Charlie says she has a music exam the next day and needed to practise. She tries to explain to him what playing the piano means to her and how Miss Fry has changed her way of thinking – not only about the music, but also about herself. LEE pulls out a piece of paper from his pocket. It is an internal report with confidential information about the students. He reads out the report that Miss Fry has written about Charlie.

Published by Oberon Books, London

LEE

Charlie . . . (*Pulling out a piece of paper from his pocket*) Look at this .
. . I used to have a white bike and I applied excellence in keeping it
clean. I fought for it, I was up against the weather. Some of these
teachers, they don't apply so much excellence in their day to day
business, they leave things lying around. Confidential information
about students. Just cos you don't have to be the best – don't mean
you're allowed to be the worst . . . And another internal report. It
was left on the desk in the Physics room with a load of others.
Paul's sister got hold of it a few days ago . . . I won't read both
pages, just the Miss Fry one . . . Profile. Charlie Silver. Charlie is fifteen years old. Charlie's er . . . Charlie's brother was killed in a
motorbike accident twelve months ago . . . Charlie's behaviour in
class is consistently aggressive. She finds it difficult to socialise
with other children, particularly girls. She cannot concentrate and
an incident with a fire extinguisher last year confirmed that she is .
. . confirmed that she is a disruptive force, to the detriment of the
other children's progress . . . (*Turning to next page*) Blah blah blah . .
. Music Report from Miss Fry . . . I am worried about how Charlie
will react to my leaving. She has become very attached to me and I
think she will find it very hard to settle into working with a new
teacher. She is impatient with her practice and can be clumsy – but
when her wilfulness translates into enthusiasm she tries very hard
and she has recently warmed as a personality, even giving me
chocolates after lessons as a thank you. (CHARLIE *snatches it from
him*) Are you okay? . . . I tried to tell you. I'm sorry. I mean it . . . I
shouldn't have brought it. But she shouldn't have left it lying
around. It's not just you, there's a load flying around school, they
were found a few days ago, got photocopied. Charlie, she was taking you for a ride. She's a half-arsed supply teacher, making out she
was a permanent. That's what they all do – they think we're stupid
. . . (*Pause*) I could of told you at the start that you don't learn music
from a teacher. It comes from the street: Learning what joins one
beat to the next. Running lyrical rings around people who think
that reading and writing makes them the big I am. Classroom
knocks the stuffing out of you.

Tony Lumpkin
(Aged 17-20)

She Stoops to Conquer

Oliver Goldsmith

This 18th century comedy was first produced at the Theatre Royal, Covent Garden, London, in 1773. It is set in the Hardcastles' country mansion and parodies the sentimental comedies popular at that time.

The action revolves around the arranged match and courtship between the Hardcastles' daughter Kate and Young Marlow, and the practical jokes played on family and friends by TONY LUMPKIN, Mrs Hardcastle's son by a former marriage. TONY has been ordered by his mother to marry his cousin, Constance, but he wants nothing to do with her. When he discovers she is in love with Marlow's friend, Hastings, he is only too delighted to help the lovers elope together. His mother discovers the plot and insists on accompanying Constance to her Aunt Pedigree's home, 30 miles away. TONY takes charge of the coach journey, driving them round and round the neighbouring countryside, finally tipping everyone into the local duck pond. Here he describes the adventure to Hastings, whose only concern is for Constance's safety.

Published by New Mermaids

TONY

Ay, I'm your friend, and the best friend you have in the world, if you knew but all. This riding by night, by the bye, is cursedly tiresome. It has shook me worse than the basket of a stage-coach . . . Five and twenty miles in two hours and a half is no such bad driving. The poor beasts have smoked for it: rabbit me, but I'd rather ride forty miles after a fox, than ten with such varment . . . Left them? Why where should I leave them, but where I found them? . . . Riddle me this then. What's that goes round the house, and round the house, and never touches the house? . . . Why, that's it, mon. I have led them astray. By jingo, there's not a pond or slough within five miles of the place but they can tell the taste of . . . You shall hear. I first took them down Feather-bed Lane, where we stuck fast in the mud. I then rattled them crack over the stones of Up-and-down Hill – I then introduced them to the gibbet on Heavy-tree Heath, and from that, with a circumbendibus, I fairly lodged them in the horsepond at the bottom of the garden . . . No, no. Only mother is confoundedly frightened. She thinks herself forty miles off. She's sick of the journey, and the cattle can scarce crawl. So if your own horses be ready, you may whip off with cousin, and I'll be bound that no soul here can budge a foot to follow you . . . Ay, now it's dear friend, noble Squire. Just now, it was all idiot, cub, and run me through the guts. Damn *your* way of fighting, I say. After we take a knock in this part of the country, we kiss and be friends. But if you had run me through the guts, then I should be dead, and you might go kiss the hangman . . . Never fear me. Here she comes. Vanish. She's got from the pond, and draggled up to the waist like a mermaid . . . (*Enter* MRS HARDCASTLE) Alack, mama, it was all your own fault. You would be for running away by night, without knowing one inch of the way.

smoked galloped at speed
rabbit me like 'drat me', a meaningless oath
varment vermin; hence, objectionable people (first usage). He is talking about his mother and cousin
circumbendibus roundabout process
cattle stable slang for 'horses'
draggled dirtied by being dragged through wet mud
quickset hedge a hedge formed of 'quick' – i.e. living – plants

Dalton
(American – aged 16)

The Trestle at Pope Lick Creek

Naomi Wallace

First performed at the Humana Festival, Louisville, in 1998 and at the Traverse Theatre, Edinburgh, in 2001. The action takes place in a town outside a city somewhere in the United States, in present time and in flash-back.

Sixteen-year-old DALTON CHANCE is alone in a prison cell staring ahead, unable to speak. He is haunted by the image of a 17-year-old girl, Pace Creagan, who he is accused of killing. Throughout the prison scenes his jailor, Chas, comes into the cell to talk to him and try to persuade him to tell him what happened. In flash-back we see DALTON a few months earlier running to meet Pace under the trestle at Pope Lick Creek. She dares him to run the trestle with her when the train comes through at seven-ten but DALTON chickens out. They agree to just watch the train as it passes through this time – take its measure and check its steam. But one of these days, she promises him, he will run the trestle.

It is DALTON's last night in the cell. Chas tells him they're moving him the next morning as his trial is about to begin. He talks about his own son, Brett, who was a friend of Pace. He too had run the trestle and was killed by the train. As he leaves the cell DALTON calls out to him. He is ready to talk – but Chas is already out of earshot. Then he turns back to his cell, speaking to himself slowly – and finally as though to a jury, explaining what happened that last evening at Pope Lick Creek.

Published by Faber & Faber, London

DALTON

Tell them I'm ready to talk . . . (*Chas leaves*) Hey. I want to talk now. Open the door . . . I got something to say . . . (*Shouting*) Pace wanted to make the run that night. I wouldn't do it. I was afraid. No, I was angry . . . (*Turning back to his cell door*) But I didn't touch her! I was. Upside down. I was. God damn it – I told her to run it alone . . . Pace never could say no to a dare. She stood on the tracks. She was covered in sweat. I stood below the trestle. She looked small up there, near a hundred feet above me. But until she started to run, I never thought she'd do it without me . . . I could hear her footsteps. Fast, fast . . . No! No way! I won't be your fucking witness! You're warped. That's what you are. Everybody says it. (*Beat*) Stop. You better stop! . . . God damn you, Pace Creagan! (*Now he is back in the present, and he speaks calmly to us*) But I wouldn't turn around. Pace must've slowed down. And lost her speed, when she was calling to me. Pace started to run back but she knew she'd never make it. And then she turned. Even from where I was at, I could see she was shaking her head. Back and forth, like she was saying: 'No. No. No.' (*Beat*) She didn't want to die . . . And then she did something funny. Pace couldn't even swim and there was no water in the creek, but she was going to dive . . . And this time. I watched her . . . Pace lay beside the trestle. She wasn't mashed up from the fall. Only the back of her head. I started to shout at her. Called her every name I could think of. Even a few she'd taught me herself. (*Beat*) And then. And then I did something. Something I can't. I don't know. It was. Maybe. It was. Unforgivable: I knelt beside her . . . Pace never let me kiss her, like that. So I did. And she didn't try to stop me. How could she? That's what I can't forget. She once said to me, Dalton, you can't take anything from me I don't want to give you. But then she opened her mouth. She was dead. But she opened her mouth. And I kissed her, the way I'd always wanted to. And she let me. (*Beat*) She let me. (*Beat*) I have to believe that.

Audition Speeches
for Women

Rosaline
(Aged 16)

After Juliet

Sharman Macdonald

This is a BT National Connections project presented as part of the Celebration of Youth Theatre. It was first performed in the summer of 1999 at the Royal National Theatre by Cardiff High School and Strode's College Theatre Company on the Cottesloe and Olivier stages.

After the tragic deaths of Romeo and Juliet, an uneasy truce exists between the Montague and Capulet families. Benvolio, Romeo's best friend, is in love with ROSALINE, Juliet's cousin. However, ROSALINE still loves Romeo and is bent on revenge.

In this scene, it is raining. ROSALINE walks over to a pile of lilies in the corner of the piazza. Benvolio and Mercutio's twin brother Valentine watch her from the shadows. She is holding an umbrella and a single lily as she speaks to the dead Juliet.

From: Connections Series
Published by Faber & Faber, London

ROSALINE

Your spirit haunts me, Juliet.
I see more of you dead
Than I did when you were alive; . . .
We were hardly close as cousins.
You were too small, too pretty, too rich,
Too thin and too much loved for me to cope with.
'Spoilt' is the word that springs to mind
Though I don't want to speak ill of the dead.
(*She touches the stamen of the lily. Yellow nicotine pollen stains her fingers. She rubs it in*)

All a flower does is wither
It's the memories that stay for ever:
So they tell me.
So what do I recall of you?
Juliet, daddy's princess, rich,
Mummy's darling, quite a bitch.
You scratched my face once,
From here to here;
I have the scar. I have it yet.
You can see it quite clearly
In the sunlight;
A silver line.
You wanted my favourite doll.
And of course you got it.
For though I was scarred, you cried.
And your nurse swooped down
And took the moppet from me.
Spanked me hard for making you unhappy;
Gave my doll to you, her dearest baby.
Later you stole my best friend;
Wooed her with whispers;
Told her gossip's secrets;
Gave her trinkets, sweetmeats.
Later still, you took my love
And didn't know you'd done it;
Then having taken him
You let him die . . .
Daddy's princess could not die.
She would be there at her own funeral
To watch the tears flow
And hear her praises sung.
So you haunt me . . .
Here. This is the last flower
You'll get from me.
Death flowers have the sweetest scent.
(*She casts the flower down. Shrugs*)
That's that bit done.

Agnes
(Young)

Agnes of God

John Pielmeier

First presented in a staged reading at the Eugene O'Neill Playwrights Conference in 1979 at the Actors Theatre of Louisville in 1980. It opened on Broadway at the Music Box Theatre in 1982.

Doctor Martha Livingstone has been appointed by the Court to assess AGNES, a young nun accused of killing her new-born baby. AGNES is a simple girl who has spent most of her life in the convent with little or no contact with the outside world. She denies all knowledge of a baby. The Mother Superior objects strongly to her being questioned and applies to have the Doctor taken off the case, but eventually AGNES agrees to submit to hypnosis in order to build up a picture of what happened to her.

In this earlier scene, Doctor Livingstone asks AGNES how babies are born.

Published by Samuel French, US

AGNES

I don't know what you're talking about! You want to talk about the baby, everybody wants to talk about the baby, but I never saw the baby, so I can't talk about the baby, because I don't believe in the baby! . . . No! I'm tired of talking! I've been talking for weeks! And nobody believes me when I tell them anything! Nobody listens to *me*! . . . Where do *you* think babies come from ? . . . Well, I think they come from when an angel lights on their mother's chest and whispers into her ear. That makes good babies start to grow. Bad babies come from when a fallen angel squeezes in down there, and they grow and grow until they come out down there. I don't know where good babies come out. (*Silence*) And you can't tell the difference except that bad babies cry a lot and make their fathers go away and their mothers get very ill and die sometimes. Mummy wasn't very happy when *she* died and I think she went to hell because every time I see her she looks like she just stepped out of a hot shower. And I'm never sure if it's her or the Lady who tells me things. They fight over me all the time. The Lady I saw when I was ten. I was lying on the grass looking at the sun and the sun became a cloud and the cloud became the Lady, and she told me she would talk to me and then her feet began to bleed and I saw there were holes in her hands and in her side and I tried to catch the blood as it fell from the sky but I couldn't see any more because my eyes hurt because there were big black spots in front of them. And she tells me things like – right now she's crying 'Marie! Marie!' but I don't know what that means. And she uses me to sing. It's as if she's throwing a big hook through the air and it catches me under my ribs and tries to pull me up but I can't move because Mummy is holding my feet and all I can do is sing in her voice, it's the Lady's voice, God loves you! (*Silence*) God loves you. (*Silence*) . . . I don't want to talk anymore, all right? I just want to go home.

Joni
(Aged 16)

Ancient Lights

Shelagh Stephenson

First performed at the Hampstead Theatre Club in November 2000 and set in a country cottage in Northumberland at Christmas, where Bea has invited her oldest friends – Kitty, Tom Cavallero and Tom's girlfriend, Iona – to spend the holiday with her and her new lover, Tad.

Tom is a Hollywood actor and Iona is making a documentary film about his life. Bea's daughter, JONI, is also staying over Christmas but would much rather be with her friends in Shepherd's Bush. Nevertheless, she is anxious to be part of the filming.

In this scene it is two o'clock in the morning and JONI is playing out an imaginary scene in which she is being interviewed about her 'first film role'. She is posing by a chair in her nightdress, trying to look provocative. She is interrupted by Tom before she has completed her 'interview' and dashes out of the room, mortified.

Published by Methuen Drama

JONI

(Lights up, later. Two a.m. Spotlight on JONI *posing by the chair in her nightdress. Wild applause, wolf-whistles, camera bulbs flashing. Screen images washing over the set. She strikes a series of provocative poses as the applause dies down)*

Yeah, I'm really really happy that the truth's out at last. Yeah, he gave me this ring. *(She holds out her hand)* It belonged to his mother, so you know, it seemed right. Right, it's incredible, I know, my first film and I'm nominated for an Oscar, I can't believe it, it's been an amazing year. Well, I've known Tom since I was tiny, so I've never been in awe of him or anything, and getting the film was nothing to do with our relationship because I'd already got the part before all this happened. Yeah, I met Iona a couple of times, and it was really terrible about the car crash and everything, but I think the relationship was more or less over by then. Decapitated. She never knew what hit her. I think I probably helped him to get over it. Well, it takes a bit of getting used to being over here in Beverly Hills with all the palm trees and everything, it's not much like Hammersmith, I can tell you. And getting mobbed by fans and not being able to leave the house. I've had a couple of stalkers, you know, the usual, God it's so boring. I can't go places like the supermarket any more, but we have staff and everything. Would I take my clothes off on film? I think that's a very difficult question, but yes, if the part demanded it –
(Lights change abruptly as TOM *comes in, still in his bathrobe, clutching his mobile phone and a glass of whisky. He's sniffing, as if he's taken coke, and is obviously mid-conversation)*
Tom . . . I was just going to bed, goodnight – *(She dashes out, mortified)*.

Mabel Chiltern
(Young)

An Ideal Husband

Oscar Wilde

This society comedy was first performed in 1895 at the Haymarket Theatre and is set in fashionable London.

The 'Ideal Husband' of the title is Sir Robert Chiltern, Under Secretary for Foreign Affairs, who – having in his youth sold private information about a transaction contemplated by the Government of the day – is now being threatened with exposure by the unscrupulous Mrs Cheveley. He is saved from disgrace by the intervention of his friend, Lord Goring.

MABEL CHILTERN is Sir Robert's high-spirited young sister, who throughout the play is being relentlessly pursued by her brother's secretary, Tommy Trafford, but finally accepts a proposal of marriage from Lord Goring.

In this scene, MABEL is complaining to her sister-in-law, Lady Chiltern, about Tommy's latest proposal. Lady Chiltern protests that Tommy is the best secretary her brother ever had. He has a brilliant future before him.

Published by New Mermaids

MABEL CHILTERN

Gertrude, I wish you would speak to Tommy Trafford . . . Well, Tommy has proposed to me again. Tommy really does nothing but propose to me. He proposed to me last night in the music-room, when I was quite unprotected, as there was an elaborate trio going on. I didn't dare to make the smallest repartee, I need hardly tell you. If I had, it would have stopped the music at once. Musical people are so absurdly unreasonable. They always want one to be perfectly dumb at the very moment when one is longing to be absolutely deaf. Then he proposed to me in broad daylight this morning, in front of that dreadful statue of Achilles. Really, the things that go on in front of that work of art are quite appalling. The police should interfere. At luncheon I saw by the glare in his eye that he was going to propose again, and I just managed to check him in time by assuring him that I was a bimetallist. Fortunately I don't know what bimetallism means. And I don't believe anybody else does either. But the observation crushed Tommy for ten minutes. He looked quite shocked. And then Tommy is so annoying in the way he proposes. If he proposed at the top of his voice, I should not mind so much. That might produce some effect on the public. But he does it in a horrid confidential way. When Tommy wants to be romantic he talks to one just like a doctor. I am very fond of Tommy, but his methods of proposing are quite out of date. I wish, Gertrude, you would speak to him, and tell him that once a week is quite often enough to propose to anyone, and that it should always be done in a manner that attracts some attention . . . I must go round now and rehearse at Lady Basildon's. You remember we are having *tableaux*, don't you? The Triumph of something, I don't know what! I hope it will be triumph of me. Only triumph I am really interested in at present. (*Kisses* LADY CHILTERN *and goes out; then comes running back*) Oh, Gertrude, do you know who is coming to see you? That dreadful Mrs Cheveley, in a most lovely gown. Did you ask her? . . . I assure you she is coming upstairs, as large as life and not nearly so natural.

Linda
(East Anglia – aged 15)

Apart from George

Nick Ward

First staged in a private performance at the National Theatre Studio in 1987, and then at the Traverse Theatre for the Edinburgh Festival prior to a national tour and production at the Royal Court Theatre Upstairs.

This is a tragedy of a small family without hope living in the Fens of East Anglia. George and Pam and their daughter LINDA are unable to communicate with each other or articulate their feelings. George has worked most of his life for John Grey the local landlord, and the only man able to give employment in the area. When times become hard, George is one of the first to be laid off and Pam is forced to work as a cleaner in Mr Grey's large house. This only increases George's sense of uselessness. LINDA has been physically abused by both her parents and now refuses to even talk to her father. When the local priest discovers George prostrate across the church aisle, he tries to help him. But even he has lost the ability to communicate with his parishioners. Eventually George hangs himself from the water pipe in the kitchen.

After the funeral Pam and LINDA talk to the audience. Pam is unable to grieve but acknowledges that she will be lonely without George. LINDA is glad her father is dead. The nightmare is over now and perhaps eventually she can forget. She speaks to her mother just once, but only to tell her that she will be going away.

Published by Faber & Faber, London

LINDA

(*To audience*) I'm glad he's fucking dead . . . Won't tell no one though . . . Not her neither . . . Don't have to tell no one now . . . Won't happen no more . . . Like the times before. Could never say nothing and I don't have to 'cause it were wrong, always knew that. Could never tell her. I'm glad he's dead . . . No more . . . What if he would never go away? What if he were to haunt me . . . ? Maybe if I don't think no more, he'll be dead in my head an' all . . . I want him to fuck off out me head . . . I'm going away soon, all right? (*Pam nods*) . . . (*To audience*) Screaming stops . . . Not a sound . . . No noise now . . . Breathing, all inside . . . Heart sound, inside – not a sound outside . . . after screams, nothing just outside me . . . Where they gone . . . ? No door sound, no slam . . . Breathing tight, inside, not out . . . Dots have gone, turned to shapes, very dark . . . heart sounds, thump, thump, thump . . . Not a word – nothing heard . . . Wide awake, in the ground . . . Lying still . . . Where's he gone . . . ? Sleep time . . . Creaking stair, turning right or turning left? Thump, thump. Where's she gone? Not a sound . . . And I'm lying there praying, 'Please God, don't let him come' . . . Flash of light from the road, someone else, other folk . . . Shapes come back . . . Ghosts are people that was unhappy when they died . . . What if he would never go away? Keep coming back? He were unhappy, else he wouldn't have done it.

Thomasina
(Aged 13–17)

Arcadía

Tom Stoppard

First presented at the Lyttleton Theatre, Royal National Theatre, in 1993.

The action takes place in Sidley Park, a large country house in Derbyshire, and shuttles back and forth between the early 19th century and the present day, as the landscape outside changes from Lady Croom's orderly Capability Brown grounds to a romantic chaos created by her landscape artist, 'Culpability Noakes'.

In a Regency room, overlooking the work, sits Lady Croom's brilliant daughter, THOMASINA, and her handsome tutor, Septimus Hodge. Their lessons are constantly interrupted by, among others, Lady Croom and Ezra Chater, a minor poet determined to exact satisfaction from Septimus for seducing his wife. Almost two hundred years later, in the same room, a mathematician, a biographer and an academic attempt to unravel the events of 1809.

It is 1809. THOMASINA sits at her table overlooking the garden, studying a sheet of paper – a 'Latin unseen' lesson she is having difficulty with. Her tutor, Septimus Hodge, is reading a letter, while Jellaby the butler waits for a reply. Plautus the tortoise, used throughout the play as a paperweight, sits on a pile of papers on the table between them. Without looking up, Septimus asks her why she has stopped. Slowly she begins to read aloud, while Septimus peels an apple, offering pieces to Plautus as he corrects her translation.

Published by Samuel French, London

THOMASINA

Solio in sessa . . . in igne . . . seated on a throne . . . in the fire . . . and
also on a ship . . . *sedebat regina* . . . sat the queen . . . the wind
smelling sweetly . . . *purpureis velis* . . . by, with or from purple sails –
. . . was like as to – something – by, with or from lovers – oh,
Septimus! – *musica tibiarum imperabat* . . . music of pipes commanded
. . . the silver oars – exciting the ocean – as if – as if – amorous –
. . . *Regina reclinabat* . . . the queen . . . was reclining – *praeter descrip-
tionem* – indescribably – in a golden tent . . . like Venus and yet more –
. . . Who is the poet? . . . Known to me? . . . I know who it is, it is your
friend Byron . . . Mama is in love with Lord Byron . . . It is not
nonsense. I saw them together in the gazebo. (*Septimus's pen stops
moving, he raises his eyes to her at last*) Lord Byron was reading to her
from his satire, and Mama was laughing, with her head in her best
position . . . She is vexed with Papa for his determination to alter the
park. But that alone cannot account for her politeness to a guest.
She came downstairs hours before her custom. Lord Byron was
amusing at breakfast. He paid you a tribute, Septimus . . . He said
you were a witty fellow, and he had almost by heart an article you
wrote about – well, I forget what, but it concerned a book called
'The Maid of Turkey' and how you would not give it to your dog
for dinner . . .You are churlish with me because Mama is paying
attention to your friend . . . Is it Cleopatra? – I hate Cleopatra! . . .
Everything is turned to love with her. New love, absent love, lost
love – I never knew a heroine that makes such noodles of our sex.
It only needs a Roman general to drop anchor outside the window
and away goes the empire like a christening mug into a pawn shop.
If Queen Elizabeth had been a Ptolemy, history would have been
quite different – we would be admiring the pyramids of Rome and
the great Sphinx of Verona . . . But instead, the Egyptian noodle
made carnal embrace with the enemy who burned the great library
of Alexandria without so much as a fine for all that is overdue. Oh,
Septimus! – can you bear it? All the lost plays of the Athenians! Two
hundred at least by Aeschylus, Sophocles, Euripides – thousands of
poems – Aristotle's own library brought to Egypt by the noodle's
ancestors! How can we sleep for grief?

Paribanou
(Young)

The Champion of Paribanou

Alan Ayckbourn

First performed at the Stephen Joseph Theatre, Scarborough, in 1996.

Murganah, the Vizier's daughter, loves Ahmed, the Sultan's youngest son, whom she has known since she was a child. When the Princess Nouronnihar arrives to choose one of the Sultan's three sons for a husband, Murganah fears the Princess will select Ahmed and invokes the help of dark, supernatural forces to keep him. Then he meets and falls in love with Paribanou and Murganah seeks a terrible revenge.

Early in the play, Ahmed and his older brothers – under pressure from the Sultan their father – are competing for the hand of the Sultan's daughter, the beautiful Princess Nouronnihar. None of them wants to marry her and she in turn has no interest in them, so she devises an impossible quest for them – to bring her 'an object from beyond her wildest dreams'. When this fails the Vizier suggests 'the test of the arrows', where they have to fire an arrow up into the Mountain of Storms and, having done this, find the arrow and bring it back. Ahmed's arrow lands much further than his brothers' – an unbelievable distance, seemingly blown by the wind. As he climbs the mountain to retrieve it, the wind increases to a blizzard and he loses his foothold. A giant figure appears through the snow, lifts him up and carries him to the Palace of Paribanou.

In this scene PARIBANOU introduces herself and welcomes Ahmed to her palace.

Alan Ayckbourn: *Plays 2*
Published by Faber & Faber, London

PARIBANOU

My name is Paribanou . . . (*Gently*) Sit down. We have much to talk about. But first I must explain a little. You are owed that. Do you like fairy tales, Ahmed? . . . Listen to this one. And pay attention. Once upon a time there were two children. A sister and a brother. Their mother had died when they were very young and as a result the brother's behaviour was often very wild. They were brought up by their father, a good and powerful wizard in the most happy of kingdoms. One day it happened that the father had to leave them in order to make a journey. He left them in the care of the servants and before he went he bade them to be good and well behaved during his absence. If they were good, he said, when he returned he would reward them with wonderful gifts. And it happened that while he was away, although the daughter obeyed her father, the brother did not. Instead he meddled with his father's spell books, and not only tormented his sister but was cruel to the servants. In fact, he became so wild and uncontrollable that when the father returned the palace was all but in ruins. For by then the son, in his search for wealth and power, had sold his very soul to Schaibar himself . . . Schaibar, the Stranger from the Darkness who seeks to lead us all into that same Darkness. Anyway, the wizard could do nothing, realizing he had lost his only son for ever. And he became first sad and then angry with his daughter for just feebly standing by and doing nothing to stop her brother. And her punishment was to remain in a beautiful but lonely cave high on a mountain. A prison she could never leave until she learnt to stand up for what is right and to oppose all that is bad. And here she has remained to this day. Alone with only Nasuh for company. You are the first visitor this place has ever seen, Ahmed. Welcome.

Nicola
(Leicester – teenage)

(ity Sugar

Stephen Poliakoff

First presented at the Bush Theatre, London ,in 1975 and then at the Comedy Theatre, London, in the following year.

The action takes place in the Sound Studio of a commercial radio station in Leicester, where disc-jockey Leonard Brazil is running a competition for his teenaged listeners. The coveted prize is to meet one of the boys from the pop group, The Yellow Jacks, at their concert in Leicester, and then to travel to London with them and stay there for four days at the expense of the studio. One of the 'phone-in' contestants is NICOLA DAVIES, who works at the local supermarket.

In this scene NICOLA has been brought into the studio. She has fought her way through the preliminary stages of the contest and has reached the final. So far she has answered most of the questions correctly and is neck-to-neck with the other finalist, Jane. She is seated in front of the microphone and Leonard asks her to talk for one minute on 'the last pop concert she went to'.

Published by Samuel French, London

NICOLA

The last – the last pop concert I went to . . . it was here in Leicester – (*she swallows*) – and Ross and the group were playing, and I queued to get in for a long time . . . I don't know, not . . . We queued for a day and a night, I think – it was a bit wet – you see, and the stone, the pavement, was very hard and cold, much harder than you think – because we slept there you see – it was all right and – and then a man came up, it was late you know then, dark and everything, and he'd come to sell us hot dogs and things, he came out there and he set up along the side of the queue, it was a very long queue, and then soon another – another came up out of the dark, and then there was another one, till there were lots and lots all along the line, really close. (*She looks up*) . . . Oh! I thought it was enough . . . Oh – and – (*lost for words, she is extremely nervous*) – and then we went inside – and the concert – and it was them of course, and it was, you know – well it was all squashed – and some people rushed up and fought to get close – and there was a bit of biting, and that sort of thing, when they called out to us; they seemed a long way off – a very long way away, in their yellow and everything. They weren't very loud – but they made you feel – I felt something come up, you know, a little sort of . . . (*A second of slightly clenched feeling*) I got, you know, a bit worked up inside – they were moving very slowly on the stage like they'd been slowed down, made me feel strange – then they held things up, waved it at us, smiling and everything, they waved yellow scarves, Ross had a bit of yellow string he waved. I think it was, a bit of yellow rope, and I half wanted to kick the girl in front of me or something because I couldn't see; all the way through I had to look at her great back, pressed right up against it. I remember I half wanted to *get at it*. Move it. And I nearly dropped a ring. (*Pulling at her finger*) I'd been pulling at, put it on specially. (*Very nervously*) If you drop anything it's gone for ever, you know – can't bend down if you're standing – and if you drop yourself – then you'd be gone. When you rush out at the end, you can see all the millions of things that have been dropped shining all over the floor, nobody gets a chance to pick them up. And then it was finished – you know, the concert, and I came outside. It was cold, I was feeling a bit funny. Just walked along out there and I thought maybe I was bleeding. I looked but I wasn't. Some people like to be after a concert, but I wasn't.

Linda
(Aged 18)

Enter a free Man

Tom Stoppard

First performed at the St Martin's Theatre in 1968.

George Riley is the 'Free Man' of the title – free from any sense of responsibility. He refuses to draw his unemployment money on the excuse that he is self-employed – as an inventor. But all his inventions come to nothing, the latest being a bottle opener that can't open a bottle and a 'use again envelope' that is sticky on both sides. When she was younger his daughter, LINDA, was proud to have an inventor as a father. Now she is fed up having to provide him with pocket money each week.

In this scene, she is complaining about the situation to her long-suffering mother, when George comes downstairs with his case packed and announces that he is leaving home.

Published by Faber & Faber, London

LINDA

Try to be charitable; I *am* a charity, I work at it full-time – You and me, we're the Society for the Preservation of George Riley! God, if his father hadn't died, he wouldn't even have a house to live in! . . . (*Getting up*) Gentleman George . . . (*At door*) Dad! Well, I hope he's calmed down since yesterday. I don't like waiting for the balloon to pop in his face. It's bad for my nerves . . . I'm not unkind. I mean I don't feel unkind. Funny thing is I'm more embarrassed than he is when he comes back from his little outings. I never know what to say . . . (*Turns and yells*) And wash your hands! If he was honest he'd come down and say, 'I've decided that some people are cut out to make a living and some people are cut out to lie in bed, and I'm the bed type so I'll be upstairs if you want me and if you're not doing

anything at four o'clock I'll have a cup of tea . . . Two lumps.'
Instead of that, he sits up there doing damn all. It's a situation, isn't
it? . . . Oh, I'm sure it passes the time very nicely. But it's driving
him half-barmy . . . You can't expect me to be sentimental about
him. I mean, life hasn't been like a National Savings advert, has it?
All the happy family round the fire and the ruddy spaniel chewing
the slipper. (*Pause*) Anyway, I don't mean he's mad or anything. If
he was *Lord* Riley he'd be called eccentric. But he's just plain old
George. So he's half-barmy . . . He's getting worse and personally I
don't think we're helping him by treating it all as normal . . . (*Pause*)
Shall I call him again? . . . (*Goes to open the door. Gets to the door just
as* RILEY *comes downstairs. He is wearing his best suit, clean shirt, tie.
He carries in one arm a briefcase and drawing-board with a coat over his
arm. The other hand is holding a large battered suitcase. The effect is
spoiled by carpet slippers*) Oh no! . . . He's packed! . . . I told you it'd
get out of hand. He's got all his gear now . . . Oh, Dad! Don't make
a thing of it. We apologise. I apologise . . . (*She comes close and speaks
with a strained gentleness*) Listen, dad – father – you don't have to go
this time. You really don't. You don't have to prove anything for us.
Just stay and don't bother, don't worry about having to prove anything – will you? – Just stay and be like other people. Put that case
back, and we'll have our dinner, and go for a walk if you like, and
tomorrow I'll go to the Labour Exchange with you and you can register. It's only signing your name. And you'll get money, every
week, if you just *register*, and maybe they'll find you something you
really like, and you'll get more money, and if you *don't* like it you
don't have to *do* it, and you *still* get money – it's the Government –
it's all there – official, do you see? Please? . . . (*Losing her gentleness
now*) Dad, if you go this time, I swear, I promise, you won't get any
more pocket-money – ever – if you don't register I'm not going to
give it to you, for your own good as well as ours – I swear it, if you
don't stay home, now.

Margaret Knox
(Aged 18)

Fanny's First Play

George Bernard Shaw

First performed at the Little Theatre in the Adelphi in 1911. It is a play within a play.

Fanny, a sheltered young girl brought up in Italy, has been sent to Cambridge to complete her education. Now she has written a play and for her birthday asks her father to arrange a private showing to an invited audience including four drama critics, but concealing the fact that she is the author. The play questions middle-class morality, suggesting that 'the young had better have their souls awakened by disgrace, capture by the police, and a month's hard labour, than drift from their cradles to their graves doing what other people do for no other reason than that other people do it, and know nothing of good and evil'. Her father is shocked. By the end of the performance, one of the critics has guessed quite correctly that the heroine, 'MARGARET', is in fact based on Fanny herself.

In the play MARGARET KNOX, the daughter of a respectable shopkeeper and his deeply religious wife, fails to return home after attending a prayer meeting with her Aunt. A fortnight later she walks in accompanied by a young French marine officer. She announces that she has been in Holloway Gaol where she was sent for assaulting a policeman and knocking out two of his teeth. Her parents are upset – she has brought disgrace on the family.

In this scene she is alone with her mother, who is trying to reason with her. MARGARET makes light of the incident: she had enjoyed the experience. Mrs Knox says she hates to see her daughter so hardened.

This edition published in 1921 by Constable and Company Ltd, London
Re-issued by Penguin in 1987

MARGARET

I'm not hardened, mother. But I can't talk nonsense about it. You see, it's all real to me. I've suffered it. I've been shoved and bullied. I've had my arms twisted. I've been made to scream with pain in other ways. I've been flung into a filthy cell with a lot of other poor wretches as if I were a sack of coals being emptied into a cellar. And the only difference between me and the others was that I hit back. Yes I did. And I did worse. I wasn't ladylike. I cursed. I called names. I heard words that I didn't even know that I knew, coming out of my mouth just as if somebody else had spoken them. The policeman repeated them in court. The magistrate said he could hardly believe it. The policeman held out his hand with his two teeth in it that I knocked out. I said it was all right; that I had heard myself using those words quite distinctly; and that I had taken the good conduct prize for three years running at school. The poor old gentleman put me back for the missionary to find out who I was, and to ascertain the state of my mind. I wouldn't tell, of course, for your sakes at home here; and I wouldn't say I was sorry, or apologise to the policeman, or compensate him or anything of that sort. I wasn't sorry. The one thing that gave me any satisfaction was getting in that smack on his mouth; and I said so. So the missionary reported that I seemed hardened and that no doubt I would tell who I was after a day in prison. Then I was sentenced. So now you see I'm not a bit the sort of girl you thought me. I'm not a bit the sort of girl I thought myself. And I don't know what sort of person you really are, or what sort of person father really is. I wonder what he would say or do if he had an angry brute of a policeman twisting his arm with one hand and rushing him along by the nape of his neck with the other. He couldn't whirl his leg like a windmill and knock a policeman down by a glorious kick on the helmet. Oh, if they'd all fought as we two fought we'd have beaten them.

Lynn
(Aged 19)

Flatmates

Ellen Dryden

First workshopped and performed by the Chiswick Youth Theatre
and published in 2000. The action takes place in a student flat in the
1990s.

Steve, a law student whose wealthy parents own the flat, rents
out two rooms to LYNN and Tom, who are studying English. Steve
is bored with Tom and tells LYNN that he has advertised his room.
A music student is interested in taking it over and will be able to
pay him more money. He wants LYNN to interview her. As LYNN
starts to protest the doorbell rings and Steve shows in Coralie and
her boyfriend, Tony. He then excuses himself and goes out, leaving
the three of them together.

LYNN is fuming. She is in no mood to interview anyone. Finally
Coralie asks if there is any point in her staying. Perhaps she should
come back later when Steve and Tom are there?

From: *Six Primroses Each and other Plays for Young Actors*
Published by First Writes Publications, London

LYNN

I ought to say I'm sorry. But I'm not. Oh! Not you. I only heard about you a few minutes ago. Steve's little joke. He is a wealthy, spoilt brat who's only interested in his stomach. When he's not eating he pushes people around for fun. Tom is a raging neurotic with a chip on his shoulder, who is busy working himself into a really juicy breakdown. They fight. Incessantly. I spend as little time as possible here because both of them, in their different ways, cling to the sweet old-fashioned notion that – deep down – I am longing to do their washing and cooking for them, and I only refuse because I'm scared that the sisters' heavy mob will come and do me over if I give way to my natural instincts and start mothering them both. Steve is reading law – officially. Tom and I are both doing English. He always hands his work in on the dot. I don't even do the work. So tutorials are a permanent embarrassment specially as I'm brighter than he is. He tries to make me work – to fulfil my potential. I refuse. He manages to miss the point about absolutely everything. Life *and* Literature. And he is scared of girls. In case they don't measure up to Mummy. Steve's scared of them too. In case they don't take food seriously . . . If you think that's a calmer atmosphere than people 'having a relationship' as you call it – getting up at lunchtime, gazing into each others' eyes instead of lunch, then disappearing for the afternoon and going for long intense walks all evening – well, you're welcome to move in right now! Rent money in advance. Strict demarcation of the 'fridge. Steve has three quarters of it. The rest of us share the one remaining shelf. Gas meter. Immersion Heater. Telephone timer. Put your calls down in the book. Launderette down the road. Delicatessen and paper shop on the corner. No credit. The Dairy stopped delivering milk because we always managed to be out when he called to be paid. Or hid. Or didn't have the money in Tom's case. (*Pause*) Is that the sort of thing you were looking for?

Pearl
(Aged in her 20s)

House and Garden

Alan Ayckbourn

First presented at the Stephen Joseph Theatre, Scarborough, in 1999 and at the Royal National Theatre on the Olivier and Lyttleton stages in August 2000. *House and Garden* is actually two plays intended to be performed simultaneously by the same cast appearing in two adjacent auditoria, and can be seen singly and in no particular order. They are about love and marriage and are at the same time funny and sad. This particular extract is taken from *Garden*.

The action takes place in a large country house and garden, belonging to businessman Teddy Platt and his wife. It is played against a background of preparations for the annual Garden Fête that afternoon, and a lunch, to which the Guest of Honour – an unknown French film actress – has been invited.

PEARL is a member of the domestic staff and described as a 'casual cleaner'. She is the daughter of the housekeeper, Izzy. Both mother and daughter live with Warn the gardener, and PEARL spends most of her working hours bringing him his lunchbox, or fighting over him with her mother. Warn takes all this for granted.

In this scene PEARL brings Warn his elevenses. Warn is feeling the grass and looking up at the sky. Throughout PEARL's dialogue he shows little or no reaction apart from sniffing or making the odd grunt.

Published by Faber & Faber, London

PEARL

Here. Brought you your 'levenses. Busy today. Got all them people coming to lunch. Doing me silver service. I nearly got it off. 'Less we have sprouts. I'm all over the place with bloody sprouts. I can do carrots. If they're cut long, you know. And beans. I'm alright with beans now. I've mastered beans. Runner beans. Not them broad buggers, they're right bastards. I had 'em everywhere last time. We were pickin' them up for months. I don't know why they don't bung it all on the plate and have done with it. Like normal people . . . Bloody garden fêtes, eh? Bet you're looking forward to it, in't yer? In't yer? You love 'em, don't you? Eh? Make your bloody year, don't they? All your lawns churned up. People parking all over your verges. Bloody pig got loose last year, remember? Dug up half the bloody veg. I hope we have that army again, they're alright. Big lads shooting each other every which way. Nuclear war they'd be off like bloody rabbits, wouldn't they? . . . Got a film star today. French one. She were in a film. The *Unex* . . . *Unin* . . . *Uninspiring* . . . I don't know. I never seen it. She gets blown up early on. Deirdre told me. But she's good while she lasts. You ought to clean this pond out. It's disgustin'. Breeding ground for things is this. You want to get a stick and clean it out.

Angela
(Northern – aged 16)

Like a Virgin

Gordon Steel

First performed by the Hull Truck Theatre Company at the
Dovecote Arts Centre, Stockton-on-Tees, in 1995, at the Edinburgh
Festival and then on a nationwide tour. It is set in Middlesborough.

ANGELA and her friend, Maxine, are besotted with Madonna.
They play truant from school, form a band, have numerous
boyfriends and dream of becoming famous very soon. Then
ANGELA becomes unwell. The doctor diagnoses Myeloid
Leukemia and she is put on chemotherapy. She is warned she may
lose her hair and buys herself a Madonna-style wig. Maxine says it
looks awful.

In this scene the girls are in ANGELA's bedroom. Maxine is
ecstatic. Jamie Powers, the boy she's been crying her eyes out over,
has phoned her and, what's more, invited her back to his house
while his mam and dad are out. She wants to go down the pub and
celebrate, but ANGELA doesn't feel like it. Maxine tells her to stop
feeling sorry for herself – it's difficult but she has to make the most
of it. She must get out and try to live a bit.

Published by Oberon Books, London

ANGELA

No, you go. I don't feel up to it . . . I've got to live a bit. Maxine, I'm dying. I don't know why but I am. I don't know why I've been picked to have such a shit-awful life. What have I done that's so bloody wrong? So you can piss off with your, 'Let's be jolly,' routine. With your, 'Let's pretend everything's alright and we'll have a laugh like we used to in the old days.' . . . Do you know something? (*Pause*) I've never had sex. I'm a virgin. Yeah I know what I said, what we said, but . . . well, they were just stories full of me, us trying to be grown-up. But I'm not gonna grow up. I'll never grow up and be a woman and have children. Why me? Why the fucking hell does it have to be me? It's not fair. How would you feel if someone told you that you were gonna die? Come on, it's not easy is it? YOU ARE GOING TO DIE. You have got four weeks to live. What are you going to do? (*Pause*) It's not easy, is it, and people are so full of understanding . . . so full of shit. 'I'd go on holiday, I'd travel.' What is the point in spending your time in strange lands with strange people? So you'll have lots of happy memories and photographs to look back on. When? I haven't got time, I'm dying. What's the point in laying on a beach getting a tan? So I'll look good in my coffin. So people will be able to gork into my coffin with . . . with . . . tear-stained eyes and say . . . 'She looks really good' . . . 'She's the best suntanned corpse I've ever seen' . . . Well, they can all fuck off. Sometimes I feel as though I should have dignity and write poems and raise money for charity an' all that . . . Be a symbol for other people to look up to. But why should I? What has anybody ever done for me? Look at you, you're pathetic stood there not wanting to say anything in case you hurt my feelings. Making excuses for me. 'It's her condition . . . It's understandable . . . She's just a bit down.' Well don't patronise me. Tell me to fuck off. Slap me. Go on. (*She pushes MAXINE*) Go on. (*She pushes her again*) Go on, do something.

Girleen
(Irish/Galway – aged 17)

The Lonesome West

Martin McDonagh

Presented at the Royal Court Theatre in 1997 as part of the Leenane Trilogy and set in Leenane, Galway.

Two brothers, Coleman and Valene, live side by side in an old farmhouse. They are forever quarrelling, even becoming violent as the poteen – supplied to them by GIRLEEN's father – takes hold of them. A young priest, Father Welsh, unable to cope with the slaughtering and suicide among his parishioners, also finds solace in drink. He tries to settle the differences between the two brothers but it's a hopeless task. And they in turn try to cheer him up by pointing out the good he has done in the parish. Even GIRLEEN does her best to joke him out of his 'crisis of faith'. After all, he does train the 'under-twelves' – a notoriously rough girls' football team.

In this scene Father Welsh is sitting on a bench on a lakeside jetty at night. He has just come back from conducting the funeral service for Tom Hanlon who drowned himself in the lake. He has a pint in his hand. GIRLEEN enters. She sits down beside him. She congratulates him on his sermon and he tells her he is leaving the parish.

Published by Dramatists Play Service, Inc.

GIRLEEN

Father. What are ya up to? . . . That was a nice sermon at Thomas's today, Father . . . I was at the back a ways. (*Pause*) Almost made me go crying, them words did . . . I'd be saying you've had a few now, Father? . . . I wasn't starting on ya . . . I wasn't starting at all on ya. I do tease you sometimes but that's all I do do . . . I do only tease you now and again, and only to camouflage the mad passion I have deep within me for ya . . . (*Welsh gives her a dirty look. She smiles*) No, I'm only joking now, Father . . . Ah be taking a joke will ya, Father? It's only cos you're so high-horse and up yourself that you make such an easy target . . . It's tonight you're going? . . . But that's awful quick. No one'll have a chance to wish you good-bye, Father . . . Will you write to me from where you're going and be giving me your new address, Father . . . Just so's we can say hello now and then, now . . . It's more than Thomas has killed himself here down the years, d'you know, Father? Three other fellas walked in here, me mam was telling me . . . You're not scared because you're pissed to the gills. I'm not scared because . . . I don't know why. One, because you're here, and two, because . . . I don't know. I don't be scared of cemeteries at night either. The opposite of that, I do *like* cemeteries at night . . . (*Embarrassed throughout*) It's because . . . even if you're sad or something, or lonely or something, you're still better off than them lost in the ground or in the lake, because . . . at least you've got the *chance* of being happy, and even if it's a real little chance, it's more than them dead ones have. And it's not that you're saying, 'Hah, I'm better than ye,' no, because in the long run it might end up that you have a worse life than ever they had and you'd've been better off as dead as them, there and then. But at least when you're still here there's the *possibility* of happiness, and it's like them dead ones know that, and they're happy for you to have it. They say 'Good luck to ya.' (*Quietly*) Is the way I see it anyways . . . I'll be carrying on the road home for meself now, Father. Will you be staying or will you be walking with me? . . . See you so, Father . . . If you let me know where you get to I'll write with how the under-twelves get on tomorrow. It may be in the *Tribune* anyways. Under 'Girl decapitated in football match'.

Sally
(Aged 20)

Love on the Dole

Ronald Gow and Walter Greenwood

First performed at the Manchester Repertory Theatre in 1934 and in London at the Garrick Theatre in 1935, it is set in Hanky Park, Salford, Lancashire.

In Hanky Park in the 1930s, unemployment is high. The Hardcastles are a respectable working-class family. But Mr Hardcastle is on the dole, his wife takes in washing and their son, Harry, works in a machine shop for a few shillings a week. Only their daughter SALLY, who works in the local mill, brings in a proper wage.

SALLY meets and falls in love with Larry Meath and they plan to get married and move away from Hanky Park. When he is killed during a riot at a street-meeting her hopes and plans for a better future are shattered. She becomes the mistress of Sam Grundy, a prosperous bookmaker and her father turns her out of the house.

In this scene SALLY is dressed for her departure. She carries a small leather suitcase. Her father demands to know if the tales he's heard about her are true.

Published by Samuel French, London

SALLY

It's true, Mother, and I don't care who knows it. (*She crosses to R of the table*) Aye, and I'll tell you something else. It's sick I am of codging old clothes to try and make them look like something. And sick I am of working week after week and seeing nothing for it. I'm sick of never having anything but what's been in pawnshops and crawling with vermin – oh, I'm sick of the sight of Hanky Park and everybody in it . . . Who cares what folk say? There's none I know as wouldn't swap places with me if they had the chance. You'd have me wed, would you? Then tell me where's the fellow around here can afford it. Them as *is* working ain't able to keep themselves, never mind a wife. Look at yourself – and look at our Harry! On workhouse relief and ain't even got a bed as he can call his own. I suppose I'd be fit to call your daughter if I was like that with a tribe of kids at me skirts. Well, can you get our Harry a job? No, but I can. Yes, me. I've got influence now – but I'm not respectable . . . (*She crosses to the sofa, picks up her jacket and puts it on then turns to face her father*) You kicked our Harry out because he got married and you're kicking me out because I ain't. You'd have me like all the rest of the women, working themselves to death and getting nothing for it. Look at Mother! Look at her! (*Pointing*) Well there ain't a man breathing, now Larry's gone, who can get me like *that* – for him!

Frankie
(American – aged 12)

Member of the Wedding

Carson McCullers

First produced in New York in 1950 at the Empire Theatre and set in a small southern town in America in August 1945. FRANKIE is a dreamy, restless girl – one moment full of energy and the next, retreating into her fantasy world. She adores her brother Jarvis and his fiancée Janice, who are soon to be married, and has made up her mind that after the wedding she will stay with them and they will all three travel the world together. She confides her dreams to Berenice, the black cook, who warns her that two is company and three is a crowd, especially at weddings.

In this scene FRANKIE wanders out into the yard. Berenice has gone out for the evening with friends, and FRANKIE feels excluded. She calls across to her little cousin John Henry to come over and spend the night with her. John Henry wants to go out and play with the other children, but FRANKIE only wants to talk about the wedding. She is restless and disturbed.

A *New Directions* Paperback

FRANKIE

I told Berenice that I was leavin' town for good and she did not believe me. Sometimes I honestly think she is the biggest fool that ever drew breath. You try to impress something on a big fool like that, and it's just like talking to a block of cement. I kept on telling and telling and telling her. I told her I had to leave this town for good because it is inevitable. Inevitable . . . Don't bother me, John Henry. I'm thinking . . . About the wedding. About my brother and the bride. Everything's been so sudden today. I never believed before about the fact that the earth turns at the rate of about a thousand miles a day. I didn't understand why it was that if you jumped up in the air you wouldn't land in Selma or Fairview or somewhere else instead of the same back yard. But now it seems to me I feel the world going around very fast. (FRANKIE *begins turning around in circles with arms outstretched. John Henry copies her. They both turn*) I feel it turning and it makes me dizzy . . . (*Suddenly stopping her turning*) I just now thought of something . . . I know where I'm going . . . I tell you I know where I'm going. It's like I've known it all my life. Tomorrow I will tell everybody . . . (*Dreamily*) After the wedding I'm going with them to Winter Hill. I'm going off with them after the wedding . . . Shush, just now I realised something. The trouble with me is that for a long time I have been just an 'I' person. All other people can say 'we'. When Berenice says 'we' she means her lodge and church and coloured people. Soldiers can say 'we' and mean the army. All people belong to a 'we' except me . . . Not to belong to a 'we' makes you too lonesome. Until this afternoon I didn't have a 'we', but now after seeing Janice and Jarvis I suddenly realise something . . . I know that the bride and my brother are the 'we' of me. So I'm going with them, and joining with the wedding. This coming Sunday when my brother and the bride leave this town, I'm going with the two of them to Winter Hill. And after that to whatever place that they will ever go. (*There is a pause*) I love the two of them so much and we belong to be together. I love the two of them so much because they are the *we* of me.

Mary Mooney
(Aged 15–16)

Once a Catholic

Mary O'Malley

First performed at the Royal Court Theatre in 1977 and set in the Convent of Our Lady of Fatima – a Grammar School for Girls – and in and around the streets of Willesden and Harlesden, London NW10, from September 1956 to July 1957.

MARY MOONEY is a fifth-former, plain and rather scruffy but with a good singing voice. Her ambition is to become a nun. In this scene she is walking down the street with Mary McGinty and Mary Gallaher. All three are carrying heavy satchels and eating Mars Bars. Mary McGinty has refused to wear her hat and Mary Gallaher warns her that if a prefect sees her she'll get reported. McGinty doesn't care. It wouldn't worry her if she got expelled. She wonders what she'd have to do to get expelled from 'that old dump'. Perhaps she could 'make a big long willy out of plasticine and stick it on the crucifix in the chapel'. MARY MOONEY is shocked – McGinty mustn't say things like that.

[McGINTY: 'Why not? Do you reckon a thunderbolt is gonna come hurtling down from Heaven?']

Published by Amber Lane Press, Charlbury, Oxfordshire

MARY MOONEY

You mustn't say things like that . . . It doesn't happen straight away. It happens when you're least expecting it. You'd better make an Act of Contrition . . . My Dad knows this man who used to be a monk. But he couldn't keep his vows so he asked if he could be released. On the day he left he came skipping down the path with his collar in his hand. And when he opened the monastery gate he saw an alsatian sitting outside. So he hung his collar round the alsatian's neck and went on his way laughing all along the road. After that he started going into pubs every night and boasting to all the people about what he'd gone and done with his collar. Then one day he went and got married. And while he was on his honeymoon he started to get a really bad pain in his back. He was in such a terrible agony he could only walk about with a stoop. And after a while he was completely bent up double. Then he started to lose his voice. He went to loads of different doctors but none of them could do anything to help him. And now he can only get about on all fours. And when he opens his mouth to say anything he barks just like a dog. Of course it's true. He lives in Shepherds Bush . . . I bet if you were knocked down by a trolley bus this evening you'd be yelling your head off for a priest.

Sally Stokes
(Aged 17)

The Passing-Out Parade

Anne Valery

First presented at the Greenwich Theatre in 1979 and set in an ATS Barrack Room in Pontefract, Yorkshire, in early 1944.

A new group of ATS girls have arrived at the barracks. Over the next few weeks it is Sergeant Pickering's job to turn these raw recruits into 'a first class war machine' for the Passing-Out Parade. PRIVATE SALLY STOKES is one of these recruits. The eldest of a large Catholic family, she was physically abused by her father and sent to a Children's Home. She takes her religion seriously and is upset by any irreverent references to 'God' and 'Christ'. The mention of sex also upsets her.

In this scene the girls are drinking cider and singing bawdy songs. STOKES has just been sick. It is her 'first time boozing'. Private Crab leads her to a chair and sits her down. She hands her a bottle of cider, telling her to take a swig: 'Hair of the dog – it helps.'

STOKES starts to read aloud the letter she has received from Reverend Mother at the Home. Then, because she is slightly drunk, she begins to talk about her Mum and we get a glimpse of her life before she was sent away.

Note: The letter from Reverend Mother is an addition from the next scene, as STOKES's following speech is a little too short for most auditions.

Published by Samuel French, London

STOKES

(*Sits at the table and reads her letter*) 'Dear Child, Your mother has asked me to write this letter for her. She wishes to thank you for the ten shillings and to tell you she lit a candle to our Blessed Lady. You'll be sorry to hear that The Home was hit, though the good Lord saw fit to spare us. Minnie Simpson – who I believe was a special friend of yours – is now working at your old job as scullery maid. She sends the enclosed handkerchief, which she embroidered in the rest period. We all pray for you daily, that you may remain in the path of obedience in which you were raised. May God keep you. Reverend Mother. PS Father O'Brian wishes to remind you of the penance you were given.' (*She strokes the handkerchief, in tears*) . . . Me mum's a Catholic . . . (*Talking because she is drunk*) She's a proper Catholic. Don't never drink nor smoke nor swear. And she takes us to Mass – in clean socks! 'Cepting Dad of course. Says he's drinking for rest, he does. (*She hiccups*) Of a Saturday night he'd come home – you know . . . (*She looks at Crab*) Mum in with us, 'case he were too gone to notice. We'd lie there for hours sometimes – ever so still – even baby, waiting for his sound on the stair. And when he got by our door, we'd go all – little. (*She makes a gesture, crouching*) Even our mum . . . (*At Crab, scared*) Bang! (*She puts her hand to her ear*) Bang'd go the door 'gainst the dresser, mirror swinging – so we'd sees ourselves – all arms and bits – and Dad falling in shouting, 'Let's be 'aving you.' I looks through my fingers once, and he were so – so *big*! And then – sudden like – he'd – yank Mum out. Drag her all way 'cross the lino, and her clinging on to things and crying out to the Blessed Virgin to spare her. She never did. (*Closes her eyes and lies back*).

Elke
(German but with American accent – young)

Presence

David Harrower

First presented at the Royal Court Jerwood Theatre Upstairs in 2001 and set in Hamburg.

It is 1960 and memories of an horrific past – Nazi Germany and a city ablaze where human fat once ran in the gutters – still persist. A pop group from Liverpool – George, Pete and Paul – have been booked to play in the run-down Indra Club for six weeks. On their night off they meet and make friends with ELKE, a young barmaid who works at the Bar Gemini.

In this scene it is the early hours of the morning, and Paul and George are in the Bar Gemini after finishing work at the Club. It has not been a good night. ELKE comes over and sits at their table. Although she is German she speaks with an American accent. She is not happy working in Hamburg and Paul asks her why she doesn't go back to America.

Published by Faber & Faber, London

ELKE

I'm German. America's where I wanna go. America's where I wanna be. I was raised in Berlin. The American sector? That's how come the accent. I've been working on it a couple of years now, getting it right. It's pretty good, huh? . . . See, when I get to America I don't ever want to be asked about this shithole of a country again . . . You know what this city is? It's a dumping ground. It's a trashcan. All these people come here to dump their shit and spunk and vomit on us. And we stay open all night to let them do it. Because we know it's no more than we're worth . . . But you'd heard stories about how wild it was here. How anything goes? . . . You can do things here you can't do anywhere else in Europe. And we want you to. 'Cause remember what country you're in . . . Your fathers must have fought us, right? Might even have been killed by us, right? But let's not talk about that. Let's drink beer and fuck women. Let's not bring any of that other stuff up. You're British. You're too polite for that . . . Let me tell you a secret. A secret everybody knows. The club you're playing in? I do know it. You know why? It's owned by a Nazi . . . (*Silence*) I don't know his name. You work for him. You should know his name . . . He's a Nazi . . . (*Pause*) Nobody told you? . . . He wasn't SS or anything. The word is Panzer Division. Still makes him a Nazi. But it's 1960 and that's all right now. The Soviets are the evil race now. Don't matter there's hundreds of doctors, lawyers, greengrocers, club-owners in this city who are murderers. That's why I want to leave. That's why I want America. Every time I breathe in here I want to throw up. There's poison in the air. You not taste it? (*Pause. She gets up*) You guys want another beer? Something to get rid of the taste?

Lucy
(Aged 17–18)

The Rivals

Richard Brinsley Sheridan

First produced at Covent Garden in 1775 and most recently by the
Royal Shakespeare Company at the Barbican in 2000.

Lydia Languish, a wealthy young heiress, is staying with her
aunt, Mrs Malaprop, in Bath. She is in love with a penniless junior
officer, Ensign Beverley, of whom her aunt heartily disapproves.
Meanwhile Mrs Malaprop herself is involved in an exchange of
amorous correspondence with an Irish Baronet, Sir Lucius
O'Trigger. Lydia's maid LUCY, a crafty young woman out to make
a quick profit wherever she can, has been carrying the letters to and
from Sir Lucius and has led him to believe that he is in fact corresponding with Lydia.

In this scene Mrs Malaprop calls for LUCY to take yet another
letter to Sir Lucius. She warns her that being a 'simpleton' will not
excuse any betrayal of confidence. Left alone, LUCY advises all
girls of 'her station' to put on a mask of 'silliness', and recounts the
inventory of the profits made by her 'simplicity'.

Published by New Mermaids

LUCY

Ha! ha! ha! So, my dear *simplicity*, let me give you a little respite – (*altering her manner*) let girls in my station be as fond as they please of appearing expert, and knowing in their trusts; commend me to a mask of silliness, and a pair of sharp eyes for my own interest under it! Let me see to what account I have turned my *simplicity* lately – (*looks at a paper*) *For abetting Miss Lydia Languish in a design of running away with an ensign – in money – sundry times – twelve pound twelve – gowns, five – hats, ruffles, caps, etc, etc – numberless! From the said Ensign, within this last month, six guineas and a half –* about a quarter's pay! Item, *from Mrs Malaprop, for betraying the young people to her –* when I found matters were likely to be discovered – *two guineas, and a black paduasoy.* Item, *from Mr Acres, for carrying divers letters –* which I never delivered – *two guineas, and a pair of buckles.* Item, *from Sir Lucius O'Trigger – three crowns – two gold pocket-pieces – and a silver snuff-box!* – Well done, *simplicity!* – yet I was forced to make my Hibernian believe, that he was corresponding, not with the aunt, but with the niece: for, though not over rich, I found he had too much pride and delicacy to sacrifice the feelings of a gentleman to the necessities of his fortune.

paduasoy heavy corded silk; a gown of that material
divers various
crowns five-shilling pieces
pocket-pieces coins no longer current, or similar small objects, carried as lucky charms
Hibernian Irishman

Juliet
(Aged 14)

Romeo and Juliet

William Shakespeare

A tragedy written in or around 1595, and set in Verona, it is the story of two 'star-crossed lovers', Romeo Montague and JULIET CAPULET, whose tragic deaths end their families' long-standing feud.

JULIET's father has arranged a grand feast in which she is to meet Paris, a young man who has asked for her hand in marriage. But by the end of the evening JULIET has met and fallen in love with Romeo, the son of the hated Montagues. The enmity between the two families makes it impossible for them to be together and so Romeo persuades Friar Lawrence to marry them secretly at his cell.

JULIET has taken her Nurse into her confidence and sends her off early in the morning with a message for Romeo. In this scene she is waiting impatiently for her to return.

Published by Penguin Books, London

JULIET

The clock struck nine when I did send the Nurse.
In half an hour she promised to return.
Perchance she cannot meet him. That's not so.
O, she is lame! Love's heralds should be thoughts,
Which ten times faster glides than the sun's beams
Driving back shadows over louring hills.
Therefore do nimble-pinioned doves draw love,
And therefore hath the wind-swift Cupid wings.
Now is the sun upon the highmost hill
Of this day's journey, and from nine till twelve
Is three long hours, yet she is not come.
Had she affections and warm youthful blood,
She would be as swift in motion as a ball.
My words would bandy her to my sweet love,
And his to me.
But old folks, many feign as they were dead –
Unwieldy, slow, heavy and pale as lead.

(*Enter Nurse and Peter*)

O God, she comes! O honey Nurse, what news?
Hast thou met with him? Send thy man away.

Charlie
(Aged 15)

School Play

Suzy Almond

First produced at the Soho Theatre, London, in 2001.

CHARLIE SILVER is bad news in the South London comprehensive school: a problem to teachers and a bad influence on the rest of the class. Her ambitions are to front a gang, ride a motorbike and to 'mess with teachers' heads'. She boasts a long list of teachers who have given up on her account. Then Miss Fry, the new music teacher, arrives and things begin to change. CHARLIE is given countless detentions, but unknown to her 'gang' is using these detention periods to develop her suppressed musical talents.

In this scene CHARLIE is at the piano waiting for Miss Fry to arrive when her friend Lee comes bursting in. He accuses her of letting him down. She was supposed to meet him and Paul in the car park earlier that afternoon with her customised Hollister bike on which he was to ride 'a lap of honour' against his rival, Danny Chapel. CHARLIE says she has a music exam the next day and needs to practise. She tries to explain to him what playing the piano means to her and how Miss Fry has changed her way of thinking – not only about the music, but also about herself.

Published by Oberon Books, London

CHARLIE

When you do something you don't have to be the best. If everyone thought like that, there wouldn't be any buses, cos . . . cos all the bus drivers would want a Gold medal every time they pulled out the station . . . Not bus drivers . . . I mean no-one would dare look at the stars in case someone goes 'Think you're an astronaut?' . . . Miss Fry says . . . (*Pause*) You've gotta understand . . . that I gave her a hard time for ages, I was so under her skin. A few years ago she got pissed up with all the bands, I thought – yeah I'll hang out with you . . . She was mental . . . She . . . One lesson . . . you see, some lessons she didn't actually teach. And sometimes, especially at the beginning, what she did was boring, you don't wanna hear, she drones. But now and again . . . One time she was about to play a song about a lady who drowned in a river, but it was nothing to do with the lesson, it was just that she liked it. I said it sounds miserable to me, miss, but she said hang on, and she told me the story: It's a sad song, she said . . . she fought for love and she lost . . . and now her skin is white as a lily, her lips are rose red, she's still and she floats downstream. She told me to close my eyes and imagine it was a dark moonlit night and that the water was lapping around the lady, taking her in. She said that when she got to the bridge of the song there would be a special note that didn't sound like the rest of the tune. It was a high sound, extra sad, a black key near the end of the piano – and when I heard it I had to imagine it was like a shooting star bursting across the river, trying to wake up the lady. I told her I couldn't be bothered, but when she started to play . . . And at the end of the second verse, when she hit that key and the sound broke, I felt the note shoot through the roof of this room like a bullet and I saw the star burst and I wanted the lady to wake up. I couldn't wait for that note to come around again. So that she'd open her eyes.

Anna
(Aged 17–18)

Shelter

Simon Bent

Commissioned for *Connections '97* by the Royal National Theatre, this is part of a festival of 12 one-hour plays written for young people by contemporary playwrights and presented on the Cottesloe and Olivier stages in July 1997.

The action takes place in London where young people are living rough on the streets. It is set in present time and the scenes are interspersed with monologues as the characters speak to the audience, telling their stories.

In this extract ANNA is speaking to the audience. She then limps across into the scene at Charing Cross tube, supported by another girl, Leslie. John is already there eating a sandwich, and Dougie is begging for small change from passers-by. She sits and tries to take off her shoe. Dougie helps her.

Note: Here ANNA's dialogue to the audience is joined to another scene a little further on in the play.

From: *New Connections – New Plays for Young People*
Published by Faber & Faber, London

ANNA

(*Addressing the audience*) I had this one job, through an agency like, working in a hotel as a cleaner. Anyway, the manager sent me down to clean the toilets and I couldn't do it – I just stood there looking at these toilets and all the time I could hear this voice, this teacher we had at school, saying to me, 'You'll end up nothing, Glover, you'll end up a toilet cleaner,' and I kept looking at these toilets and I kept thinking, 'This is it, this is the rest of my life' – I couldn't do it, and the manager went ape, he threatened to sack us, so I told him where to stick his rotten job. I'd rather be out on the street. The money's not much worse and you haven't got some fascist shouting in your face if you don't like it . . . (*Anna sits and tries to take off her shoe. Dougie helps her*) I've been run over – flippin' shoe. I'm standing on the pavement and this bike just runs me over – . . . What's so funny then? . . . I was standing on the corner of Warren Street, talking to Lesley and Niki – . . . Are you listening to me? . . . So I'm stood there talking to Niki and Lesley, right – when all of a sudden something hits me from behind and I'm not standing any more. I'm flat out on the pavement and it feels like someone's just punched me in the ribs, like I've been hit by a sledgehammer – and I can see my bag in the road and a bus runs over it and all I can hear is Niki shouting and screaming, and I don't know what's happening and I'm lying there thinking I could've been my bag and no one cares – I get run over in broad daylight and no one cares . . . I'm in a state of shock – I'll kill the pig that did it and if I can't find him I'll go round London and slash every bike tyre in sight . . . I could've been killed, for all the difference it'd make to you two – 'Where's Anna? . . . Dead, got knocked over by a bike . . . Oh, got any fags?'

ILSE
(Teenaged)

Spring Awakening

Frank Wedekind

First performed in Germany in 1891 and in London at the Royal Court Theatre in 1965. This new version by Ted Hughes was presented by the Royal Shakespeare Company in The Pit at the Barbican, London, in 1995.

The play deals with the problems of young love and the inability of adults to talk openly to their children. The story revolves around Wendla and Moritz, who pay with their lives for their parents' moral dishonesty.

Moritz has failed to obtain a place in the Upper Class at school, despite long hours of hard study. Unable to face his parents' reaction to the news he makes up his mind to kill himself. In this scene he is walking along a winding path at dusk through marshy undergrowth. ILSE suddenly appears and Moritz, startled, accuses her of sneaking up on him. ILSE has already left school and is working in town as an artist's model. She asks him if he has a hangover and he tells her he has been up all night drinking. She reminds him of their schooldays together and tells him about her present life and her adventures and narrow escapes living among the artists. She invites him home with her, but he excuses himself saying he has to get back to prepare his work for the next morning. As she leaves he calls after her, but she doesn't hear him.

Published by Faber & Faber, London

ILSE

I don't know what a hangover is. Last carnival I never got to bed or changed my clothes for three days and three nights. From the ball to the café, the Bellavista at midday, cabaret in the evening, then back to the ball. Lena was there, and Viola – remember the fat girl? Then on the third night Heinrich found me . . . He tripped over my arm. I was flat out unconscious in the snow on the street. He took me back to his place. I was there two weeks – what a ghastly fortnight that was! Mornings I had to swan about his apartment in his Persian bathrobe. Evenings it was his little black pageboy outfit. White lace at the throat, the wrists and the knees. Every day he'd photograph me in some exotic pose – Ariadne draped over the back of a sofa, or as Leda or Ganymede. Once down on all fours as a female Nebuchadnezzar. All the time he was ranting on about killing, shooting, suicide, gas. Then he'd jump up at three a.m. and come back to bed with a pistol, load it and stick it into my breast. 'Blink once,' he'd say, 'and I'll blast you wide open.' And he would have too, Moritz. He was quite capable, believe me. Then he'd put the thing in his mouth as if it were a blow-pipe. All to rouse my instinct of self-preservation. And then – ugh! The bullet would have gone straight through my backbone . . . Directly over his bed, in the ceiling, was a mirror. It made his tiny den seem to go straight up – like a tower, and very bright, like an opera house. You saw yourself hanging there in the heavens, face downwards. Every night I had the most horrible nightmares. Then I would lie awake just gritting my teeth to make the hours pass – please God, make it morning soon. Good night, Ilse. When you are asleep, do you know, my darling, you are beautiful enough to murder . . . I pray to God he's dead. One day while he was out for his absinthe, I slipped his coat on and got away down the street. Carnival time was long past and the police picked me up. So it's what am I doing in a man's coat and straight off to the police station. Then in came Nohl, Fehrendorf, Padinsky, Spuhler, Oikonomopulos, the whole Phallopia, and they bailed me out. They took me off to Adolar's in a cab. So ever since I've stuck with them. Fehrendorf is a baboon. Nohl is an arsehole. Bojokewitsch is a blockhead. Boison has no principles whatever. And Oikonomopulos is a clown. But I love them all and wouldn't hook up with anybody else, even if the rest of the world were nothing but angels and billionaires.

Heavenly
(Southern American – young)

Sweet Bird of Youth

Tennessee Williams

First presented at the Martin Beck Theatre, New York, in 1959.

Chance Wayne is an ambitious hustler. He has currently taken up with the Princess Kosmonopolis, a fading film star, whom he imagines will be able to further his film career. She accompanies him back to his home town, where he attempts to see HEAVENLY with whom he once had an affair and still loves. But, unknown to him, he has infected her with venereal disease and her father, politician Boss Finley, has sworn to have him castrated.

Chance has been trying desperately to contact HEAVENLY – driving past her house in his car and making innumerable phone calls. In this scene Boss tells his daughter he wants to have a word with her. People are talking about her – she is becoming an issue, a subject of scandal – and this could harm his political career. In turn she accuses him of sending away the boy she loved, and reminds him that his well-known affair with the notorious 'Miss Lucy' has been going on even while her mother was still alive. He denies all knowledge of this. He wants her to go out and buy herself a brand new outfit and appear on the platform with him when he addresses the 'Youth for Tom Finley' club, in 'the stainless white of a virgin' to put an end to the ugly rumours that are going around about her.

Published by Penguin Books, London

HEAVENLY

Don't give me your 'Voice of God' speech. Papa, there was a time when you could have saved me, by letting me marry a boy that was still young and clean, but instead you drove him away, drove him out of St Cloud. And when he came back, you took me out of St Cloud, and tried to force me to marry a fifty-year-old money bag that you wanted something out of – . . . and then another, another, all of them ones that you wanted something out of. I'd gone, so Chance went away. Tried to compete, make himself big as these big-shots you wanted to use me for a bond with. He went. He tried. The right doors wouldn't open, and so he went in the wrong ones, and – Papa, you married for love, why wouldn't you let me do it, while I was alive, inside, and the boy still clean, still decent? . . . (*Shouting*) You married for love, but you wouldn't let me do it, and even though you'd done it, you broke Mama's heart, Miss Lucy had been your mistress – . . . Oh, Papa, she was your mistress long before Mama died. And Mama was just a front for you. Can I go in now, Papa? Can I go in now? . . . Papa, I'm sorry my operation has brought this embarrassment on you, but can you imagine it, Papa? I felt worse than embarrassed when I found out that Dr George Scudder's knife had cut the youth out of my body, made me an old childless woman. Dry, cold, empty, like an old woman. I feel as if I ought to rattle like a dead dried-up vine when the Gulf Wind blows, but, Papa – I won't embarrass you any more. I've made up my mind about something. If they'll let me, accept me, I'm going into a convent.

117

Maire
(Donegal – young)

Translations

Brian Friel

First presented by the Field Day Theatre Company in the Guildhall, Derry, in 1980.

The action takes place in 1833 at a hedge-school in the townland of Baile Beg, an Irish-speaking community in county Donegal. Nearby there is a recently arrived detachment of the Royal Engineers, making the first ordnance survey. The play examines the effects of this operation on the lives of the local people.

The sappers have already mapped out most of the area and now Lieutenant George Yolland has been allotted the task of changing the place names into Gaelic. He is assisted by Owen, son of the Master at the School. Through Owen he meets and falls in love with MAIRE – a young girl who attends the hedge-school and works on a nearby farm.

In this scene it is evening and MAIRE arrives at the school carrying a pail of milk. She hasn't seen Yolland since the previous night and he has failed to report for work that morning. She is distraught. Yolland would never have gone away without letting her know. She begs Owen to tell her if he's heard anything.

Published by Faber & Faber, London

MAIRE

Honest to God, I must be going off my head. I'm half-way here and I think to myself, 'Isn't this can very light?' and I look into it and isn't it empty . . . Yolland left me home, Owen. And the last thing he said to me – he tried to speak in Irish – he said, 'I'll see you yesterday' – he meant to say 'I'll see you tomorrow.' And I laughed that much he pretended to get cross and he said 'Maypoll! Maypoll!' because I said that word wrong. And off he went, laughing – laughing, Owen! Do you think he's all right? What do *you* think? . . . He comes from a tiny wee place called Winfarthing. (*She suddenly drops on her hands and knees on the floor – where Owen had his map a few minutes ago – and with her finger traces out an outline map*) Come here till you see. Look. There's Winfarthing. And there's two other wee villages right beside it; one of them's called Barton Bendish – it's there; and the other's called Saxingham Nethergate – it's about there. And there's Little Walsingham – that's his mother's townland. Aren't they odd names? Sure they make no sense to me at all. And Winfarthing's near a big town called Norwich. And Norwich is in a county called Norfolk. And Norfolk is in the east of England. He drew a map for me on the wet strand and wrote the names on it. I have it all in my head now: Winfarthing – Barton Bendish – Saxingham Nethergate – Little Walsingham – Norwich – Norfolk. Strange sounds, aren't they? But nice sounds; like Jimmy Jack reciting his Homer. (*She gets to her feet and looks around; she is almost serene now. To Sarah*) You were looking lovely last night, Sarah. Is that the dress you got from Boston? Green suits you. (*To Owen*) Something very bad's happened to him, Owen. I know. He wouldn't go away without telling me. Where is he, Owen? You're his friend – where is he? (*Again she looks around the room; then sits on a stool*) I didn't get a chance to do my geography last night. The master'll be angry with me. (*She rises again*) I think I'll go home now. The wee ones have to be washed and put to bed and that black calf has to be fed . . . My hands are that rough; they're still blistered from the hay. I'm ashamed of them. I hope to God there's no hay to be saved in Brooklyn. (*She stops at the door*) Did you hear? Nellie Ruadh's baby died in the middle of the night. I must go up to the wake. It didn't last long, did it?

Pace
(American – aged 17)

The Trestle at Pope Lick Creek

Naomi Wallace

First performed at the Humana Festival, Louisville, in 1998 and at the Traverse Theatre, Edinburgh, in 2001. The action takes place in a town outside a city somewhere in the United States in present time and in flash-back.

Sixteen-year-old Dalton Chance is alone in a prison cell staring ahead, unable to speak. He is haunted by the image of a 17-year-old girl, PACE CREAGEN, whom he is accused of killing. In flash-back we see him a few months earlier running to meet her under the trestle at Pope Lick Creek. She dares him to run the trestle with her when the train comes through at seven-ten. She has done it once before on her own. Her second attempt was with her friend Brett, ending in disaster when he tripped as the train was almost on him and was killed. When Dalton refuses to run, she pulls a switchblade on him. He is unimpressed and tells her that Brett was mental and she is warped – everyone at school says so. They agree to just watch the train as she passes through – take her measure and check her steam. But one of these days she promises him, he will run the trestle.

For several days they meet at Pope Lick Creek – talking about the train and even acting out a scene where Dalton trips and the train strikes him, reducing him to bits of meat and mashed potatoes.

In the following speech PACE describes the moment leading up to Brett being struck by the train.

Published by Faber & Faber, London

PACE

You were wrong the other day. That's not what a train does to you. It doesn't mush you up in neat little pieces. This train. She's a knife. That's why we loved her. Me and Brett. This train, you've seen her. So much beauty she's breathless: a huge hunk and chunk of shiny black coal blasted fresh out of the mountain. (*Beat*) We had a good start. Me and Brett. We both could have made it. 'Course Brett, he was faster. I expected to be running behind. But Brett was worried. About me. He was stupid like that. He turned to look over his shoulder at me and he tripped. I thought he'd just jump up and keep going so I passed him right by. We'd timed it tight, and right then that engine was so close I could smell her. (*Beat*) I thought Brett was right behind me . . . I thought he was running behind me. I could hear him behind me. He didn't call out. He didn't say wait up. I didn't know. Why didn't he call out? (*There is the real sound of a whistle in the distance*) Not even a sound. Brett just sat there where he'd fallen. And then he stood up, slowly, like he had the time. He stood there looking at her, looking her straight in the face. Almost like a dare. Like: 'Go ahead and hit me.' You can't do that to a train. You can't dare a train to hit you. 'Cause it will. (*Another whistle, closer this time*) . . . Just stood there like she could pass right through him for all he cared. Like he wasn't going to flinch . . . It's not how you think it is. The train, she doesn't mush you up. An arm here. A leg here. A shoe. No. She's cleaner than that. I walked back down the tracks after the train had passed. She cut Brett in two . . . You know what I thought? Blocks. Two blocks, and maybe if I could fit the pieces back together again, he'd be. Whole.

Ruby
(Yorkshire – aged 16–17)

When We Are Married

J B Priestley

First performed at the St Martin's Theatre, London, in 1938 and most recently at the Haymarket Theatre in 1995.

The action takes place in the sitting room of Alderman Helliwell's house in Clecklewyke, a town in the West Riding, on an evening in 1908.

In this opening scene the front-door bell rings and RUBY BIRTLE, a very young 'slavey' of the period, shows in Gerald Forbes. Gerald has come to see Alderman Helliwell, but RUBY informs him he will have to wait. Alderman and Mrs Helliwell have company and they haven't finished their tea yet. Gerald is in no mood for a chat but RUBY insists on telling him all about the guests and every detail of what they are eating.

Published by Samuel French, London

RUBY

(*L of the door*) You'll have to wait, 'cos they haven't finished their tea
. . . (*Approaching, confidentially*) It's a do . . . A do. Y'know, they've
company . . . (*After nodding, going closer still*) Roast pork, stand pie,
salmon and salad, trifle, two kinds o' jellies, lemon-cheese tarts, jam
tarts, swiss tarts, sponge cake, walnut cake, chocolate roll, and a
pound cake kept from last Christmas . . . (*Seriously*) No, there's
white bread, brown bread, currant teacake, one o' them big curd
tarts from Gregory's, and a lot o' cheese . . . (*After nodding, then very
confidentially*) And a little brown jug . . . (*Still confidentially*) You
know what that is, don't you? (*She laughs*) Well, I never did! Little
brown jug's a drop o' rum for your tea. They're getting right lively
on it. (*Coolly*) But you don't come from round here, do you? . . . (*A
distant bell rings, not the front-door bell*) I come from near Rotherham.
Me father works in t'pit, and so does our Frank and our Wilfred.
(*The distant bell sounds again*) . . . (*Coolly*) It's for me. Let her wait.
She's run me off me legs to-day. And Mrs Northrop's in t'kitchen –
she can do a bit for a change. (*She crosses to* GERALD) There's seven
of 'em at it in t'dining-room – Alderman Helliwell and missus, of
course – then Councillor Albert Parker and Mrs Parker, and Mr
Herbert Soppitt and Mrs Soppitt – and of course Miss Holmes . . .
Yes, but she's stopped eating. (*She giggles*) You're courting her,
aren't you? . . . (*Coolly*) Oh – I saw you both – the other night, near
Cleckley Woods. I was out meself, with our milkman's lad . . . Now
don't look like that, I won't tell on you . . . She can't put it away like
some of 'em. I'd rather keep Councillor Albert Parker a week than
a fortnight. D'you want to see her? . . . I'll tell her. (*She turns back*)
She'd better come round that way – through t'greenhouse . . .

Audition Speeches
for Men or Women

Serpent

Back to Methuselah

George Bernard Shaw

First presented by the Theatre Guild at the Garrick Theatre, New York, in 1922. In his preface Shaw says that he has written this play as a contribution to the modern Bible.

In this first section – 'In The Beginning' – Adam and Eve are in the Garden of Eden and, curled around the branches of a great tree, is an immense SERPENT. Adam has discovered a fawn lying with its neck broken. He calls to Eve and together they try to revive the creature. It is their first experience of death and they are very frightened. As Adam goes off to throw the fawn's body into the river, the SERPENT becomes visible, glowing in wonderful new colours. It rears its head slowly and speaks seductively into Eve's ear.

Published by Penguin Books, London

SERPENT

Eve . . . It was I who whispered the word to you that you did not know. Dead. Death. Die . . . Death is not an unhappy thing when you have learnt how to conquer it . . . By another thing, called birth . . . The serpent never dies. Some day you shall see me come out of this beautiful skin, a new snake with a new and lovelier skin. That is birth . . . If I can do that, what can I not do? I tell you I am very subtle. When you and Adam talk, I hear you say 'Why?' Always 'Why?' You see things; and you say 'Why?' But I dream things that never were; and I say 'Why not?' . . . Why not be born again and again as I am, new and beautiful every time? . . . Listen. I will tell you a great secret. I am very subtle; and I have thought and thought and thought. And I am very wilful, and must have what I want; and I have willed and willed and willed. And I have eaten strange things: stones and apples that you are afraid to eat . . . I dared everything . . . I gathered a part of the life in my body, and shut it into a tiny white case made of the stones I had eaten . . . I shewed the little case to the sun, and left it in its warmth. And it burst; and a little snake came out; and it became bigger and bigger from day to day until it was as big as I. That was the second birth . . . It near-ly tore me asunder. Yet I am alive, and can burst my skin and renew myself as before. Soon there will be as many snakes in Eden as there are scales on my body. Then death will not matter: this snake and that snake will die; but the snakes will live . . . Think. Will. Eat the dust. Lick the white stone: bite the apple you dread. The sun will give life . . . Do. Dare it. Everything is possible: everything.

Puck

A Midsummer Night's Dream

William Shakespeare

A comedy written somewhere between 1595 and 1599, the action takes place in Athens as preparations are being made for the wedding of Duke Theseus and Hippolyta, Queen of the Amazons.

At the same time there is unrest in the Fairy Kingdom. The Fairy King, Oberon, has quarrelled with his Queen, Titania, over the possession of a little Indian boy whom she has taken under her protection. To punish her, Oberon sends his attendant sprite, PUCK, to find a magic flower known as 'Love in Idleness'. Oberon squeezes the juice of this flower into Titania's eyes as she is sleeping in her secret bower, so that when she awakes she will fall in love with the first thing she sets eyes on.

In a wood nearby a group of Athenian workmen, lead by Bottom the weaver, are rehearsing a play – *Pyramus and Thisbe* – to be performed before the Duke on his wedding day. As Bottom finishes his scene and walks away from his fellow actors, PUCK espies him and quickly places an ass's head on his shoulders.

In this scene PUCK returns to tell Oberon his news. Titania has woken in her secret bower as Bottom entered through a brake in the hedge and has straightaway fallen in love with 'an ass'.

Note: PUCK can take on any form and therefore can be played by man, woman or child.

Published by Penguin Books, London

PUCK

My mistress with a monster is in love.
Near to her close and consecrated bower,
While she was in her dull and sleeping hour,
A crew of patches, rude mechanicals
That work for bread upon Athenian stalls,
Were met together to rehearse a play
Intended for great Theseus' nuptial day.
The shallowest thickskin of that barren sort,
Who Pyramus presented, in their sport
Forsook his scene and entered in a brake,
When I did him at this advantage take.
An ass's nole I fixèd on his head.
Anon his Thisbe must be answerèd,
And forth my mimic comes. When they him spy –
As wild geese that the creeping fowler eye,
Or russet-pated choughs, many in sort,
Rising and cawing at the gun's report,
Sever themselves and madly sweep the sky –
So at his sight away his fellows fly,
And at our stamp here o'er and o'er one falls.
He 'Murder!' cries, and help from Athens calls.
Their sense thus weak, lost with their fears thus strong,
Made senseless things begin to do them wrong.
For briars and thorns at their apparel snatch,
Some sleeves, some hats. From yielders all things catch.
I led them on in this distracted fear,
And left sweet Pyramus translated there;
When in that moment – so it came to pass –
Titania waked, and straightway loved an ass.

Gail/Oggy Moxon
(Aged 16–17)

Teechers

John Godber

First performed by the Hull Truck Company at the Edinburgh Festival in 1987 and set in a School Hall with a wooden stage, desks and chairs.

School leavers, Salty, Hobby and GAIL, are presenting a play about life at Whitewall High – described as a comprehensive school somewhere in England, with its fair share of problems. All three play different characters, sometimes acting as narrators. In this scene GAIL plays 'Bobby Moxon' – the cock of Whitewall High – known to all and sundry as 'OGGY MOXON'. ('OGGY' can be played either as 'OGGY' himself or as Gail playing 'OGGY'.)

Note: If a male actor is playing 'OGGY' then you need to cut the lines from 'I knew that he fancied me' to 'somebody ought to drop him' and then take it up again from the line 'Oggy Moxon's speech about being hard' and continue to the end of the extract.

From: *John Godber: Five Plays*
Published by Penguin Books, London

GAIL

The cock of Whitewall High was Bobby Moxon, known to all and sundry as – Oggy Moxon. There was no doubt at all that Oggy was dangerous, all the teachers gave him a wide berth. He was sixteen going on twenty-five. Rumour had it that he had lost his virginity when he was ten and that Miss Prime fancied the pants off him . . . One Wednesday, I was stood outside one of the mobile classrooms. Mr Dean had sent me out of class. I'd told him that I thought Peter the Great was a bossy gett! And he sent me out. I'm stood there with a mood on when Oggy comes past . . . I knew that he fancied me. (*As* OGGY) What you doing? (*As* GAIL*)* Waiting for Christmas, what's it look like? (*As* OGGY) I'm having a party in my dad's pub, wanna come? Most of the third year is coming. Should be a good night . . . Might see you there . . . Wear something that's easy to get off. Your luck might be in. (*As* GAIL) I hate him . . . Somebody ought to drop him . . . Oggy Moxon's speech about being hard: I'm Oggy Moxon . . . We said you'd have to use your imaginations. I'm Oggy, I'm as hard as nails, as toe-capped boots I'm hard, as marble in church, as concrete on your head I'm hard. As calculus I'm hard. As learning Hebrew is hard, then so am I. Even Basford knows I'm rock, his cane wilts like an old sock. And if any teachers in the shit-pot school with their degrees and bad breath lay a finger on me, God be my judge, I'll have their hides. And if not me, our Nobby will be up to this knowledge college in a flash. All the female flesh fancy me in my five-o-ones, no uniform for me never. From big Mrs Grimes to pert Miss Prime I see their eyes flick to my button-holed flies. And they know like I that no male on this staff could satisfy them like me, cos I'm hard all the time. Last Christmas dance me and Miss Prime pranced to some bullshit track and my hand slipped down her back, and she told me she thought that I was great, I felt that arse, that schoolboy wank, a tight-buttocked, Reebok-footed, leggy-arse . . . I touched that and heard her sigh . . . for me. And as I walk my last two terms through these corridors of sickly books and boredom, I see grown men flinch and fear. In cookery one day my hands were all covered with sticky paste, and in haste I asked pretty Miss Bell if she could get for me an hanky from my pockets, of course she would, a student on teaching prac-tice – wanting to help, not knowing my pockets had holes and my underpants were in the wash. 'Oh, no,' she yelped, but in truth got herself a thrill, and has talked of nothing else these last two years. Be warned, when Oggy Moxon is around get out your cigs . . . And lock up your daughters . . .

Dog

The Witch of Edmonton

Thomas Dekker, John Ford & William Rowley

A tragicomedy written in 1621 and often performed at The Cockpit
in Drury Lane. One of its more recent productions was by the Royal
Shakespeare Company at the Other Place in Stratford in 1981.

Old Mother Sawyer – the Witch – has sold her soul to the devil,
who appeared to her in the shape of a black DOG, so that she might
be revenged on all those who harmed her. At the same time DOG
has befriended Cuddy, a simple village boy, who has no idea that
his friend 'Tommy' is in reality the devil in one of his many dis-
guises. Now 'Tommy' has gone missing for several days. The
Witch's powers have begun to wane and she is captured and con-
demned to hang.

In this scene DOG appears to Cuddy for the last time as a white
dog. Cuddy recognises him by his bark and stops to speak to him.
DOG boasts of his devilish exploits. He explains to Cuddy how he
lured him into Edmonton marsh when they first met, by changing
into the shape of Kate Carter, the village girl Cuddy was chasing
after.

Published by New Mermaids

DOG

Hast thou forgot me? . . . (*Barks*) I have deluded thee
For sport to laugh at. The wench thou seekst
After thou never spakst with, but a spirit
In her form, habit and likeness. Ha, ha! . . .
I'll thus much tell thee. Thou never art so distant
From an evil spirit, but that thy oaths,
Curses and blasphemies pull him to thine elbow.
Thou never tellst a lie, but that a Devil
Is within hearing it; thy evil purposes
Are ever haunted; but when they come to act,
As thy tongue slandering, bearing false witness,
Thy hand stabbing, stealing, cosening, cheating,
He's then within thee. Thou playst, he bets upon thy part;
Although thou lose, yet he will gain by thee . . .
The old cadaver of some self-strangled wretch
We sometimes borrow, and appear human.
The carcass of some disease-slain strumpet,
We varnish fresh, and wear as her first beauty.
Didst never hear? if not, it has been done.
An hot luxurious lecher in his twines,
When he has thought to clip his dalliance,
There has provided been for his embrace
A fine hot flaming Devil in her place . . .
Why? These are all my delights, my pleasures, fool . . .
Ha, ha! The worse thou heardst of me, the better 'tis.
Shall I serve thee, fool, at the self-same rate? . . .
I am for greatness now . . .
Hence silly fool,
I scorn to prey on such an atom soul.

Thou . . . thee Since the Devil's agent is giving conventional Puritan doctrine here, the speech is both polemical and satirical
twines embraces
When . . . dalliance when the Devil embraces the lecher
ducking . . . delight The use of water spaniels for duck hunting was a popular sport
atom tiny, irrelevant

Useful Addresses

The Actors' Theatre School
32 Exeter Road
London NW2 4SB
Tel: 020 8450 0371
Fax: 020 8450 1057

**Offstage Theatre and
Film Bookshop**
37 Chalk Farm Road
London NW1 8AJ
Tel: 020 7485 4996
Fax: 020 7916 8046

Tona de Brett
020 7372 6179

Sylvia Carson
020 8422 5026

Laine Theatre Arts
The Studios
East Street
Epsom KT17 1HH
Tel: 01372 724648
Fax: 01372 723775

Polka Theatre For Children
240 The Broadway
Wimbledon
London SW19 1SB

The British Library
96 Euston Road
London NW1 2DB
Tel: 020 7412 7676

The Academy Drama School
189 Whitechapel Road
London E1 1DN
Tel: 020 7377 8735

**The American Academy
of Dramatic Arts**
120 Madison Avenue
New York NY 10016
Tel: 212 686 9244
Fax: 212 679 8752

**The Royal Academy of
Dramatic Art**
62/64 Gower Street
London WC1E 6ED
Tel: 020 7373 9883

**London Academy of Music and
Dramatic Art (LAMDA)**
Tower House
226 Cromwell Road
London SW5 0SR
Tel: 020 7373 9883

Streets Alive
www.streetsalive.org.uk

The City Literary Institute
Stukeley Street
Drury Lane
London WC2B 5LJ
Tel: 020 7430 0544

Copyright Holders

After Juliet by Sharman MacDonald. Published by Faber and Faber Ltd.

Agnes of God by John Pielmeier. Copyright © 1982 by Courage Productions, Inc.

Ah! Wilderness by Eugene O' Neill. Published by Jonathan Cape. Reproduced by permission of The Random House Group Ltd.

Ancient Lights by Shelagh Stephenson. Reproduced by permission of Methuen Publishing Limited.

Another Country by Julian Mitchell. Copyright © Julian Mitchell 1982. Published by Amber Lane Press.

Apart from George by Nick Ward. Published by Faber and Faber Ltd.

Arcadia by Tom Stoppard. Reproduced by permission of PFD.

City Sugar by Stephen Poliakoff. Reproduced by permission of Methuen Publishing Limited.

An excerpt (abridged) from *Cressida* by Nicholas Wright. Published by Nick Hern Books, The Glasshouse, 49a Goldhawk Road, London W12 8QP.

Enter a Free Man by Tom Stoppard. Reproduced by permission of Grove/ Atlantic, Inc. Also reproduced by permission of Faber and Faber Ltd.

Entertaining Mr Sloane by Joe Orton. Reproduced by permission of Grove/ Atlantic, Inc. Also reproduced by permission of Methuen Publishing Limited.

Fanny's First Play by George Bernard Shaw. Reproduced by permission of The Society of Authors on behalf of the Bernard Shaw Estate.

Flatmates by Ellen Dryden. Reproduced by permission of First Writes

House and Garden by Alan Ayckbourn. Published by Faber and Faber Ltd.

Journey's End by R.C. Sherriff (Penguin Books, 1983). Copyright © R.C. Sherriff, 1983.

Like a Virgin by Gordon Steel. Reproduced by permission of Oberon Books.

Love on the Dole by Ronald Gow and Walter Greenwood. Reproduced by kind permission of Film Rights Ltd.

Madame Melville by Richard Nelson. Published by Faber and Faber Ltd.

Member of the Wedding reproduced by permission of the Lantz Agency.

Once a Catholic by Mary O'Malley. Copyright © Mary O'Malley 1978. Published by Amber Lane Press.